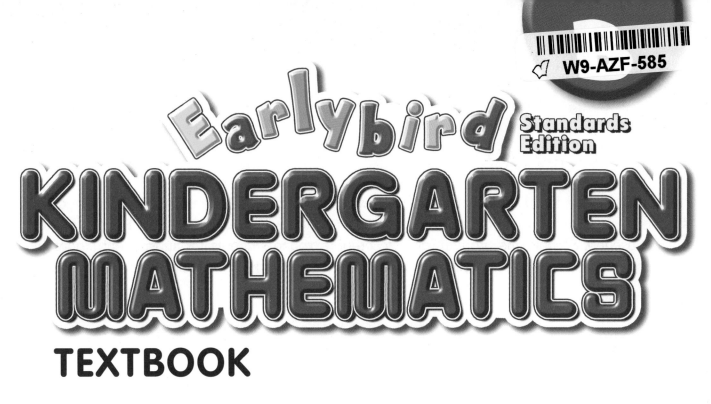

Earlybird Standards Edition
KINDERGARTEN MATHEMATICS
TEXTBOOK

Yeap Ban Har
Winnie Tan

 Marshall Cavendish
Education

PREFACE

KINDERGARTEN MATHEMATICS is a comprehensive, activity-based program designed to provide kindergarten students with a strong foundation in mathematics. Aligned with the Mathematics Framework for California Public Schools, the program aims to prepare young students for subsequent stages of mathematical thinking. In the Textbook, mathematical concepts are developed in a systematic, engaging and fun way.

Every unit comprises several lessons, each lesson has a **focused** learning outcome.

The Big Books that correlate topically to the Textbooks integrate basic mathematical concepts with well-loved children's rhymes and stories to create an enjoyable learning process.

The **teaching notes** at the bottom of the pages provide guidelines to help teachers develop lessons and mathematical concepts systematically.

Earlybird Kindergarten Mathematics (Standards Edition) is designed to form the foundation level for the Primary Mathematics (Standards Edition) series. Mathematical concepts are systematically introduced and reinforced using the **Concrete → Pictorial → Abstract** approach.

The **Concrete → Pictorial → Abstract** approach enables students to encounter math in a meaningful way through concrete activities before progressing to pictorial and abstract representations.

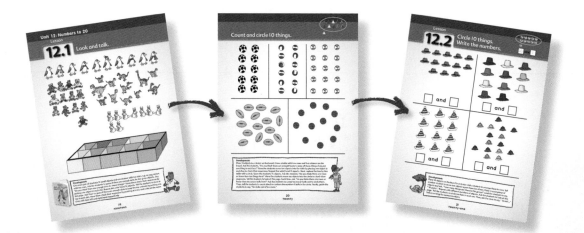

11.1

Look and talk.

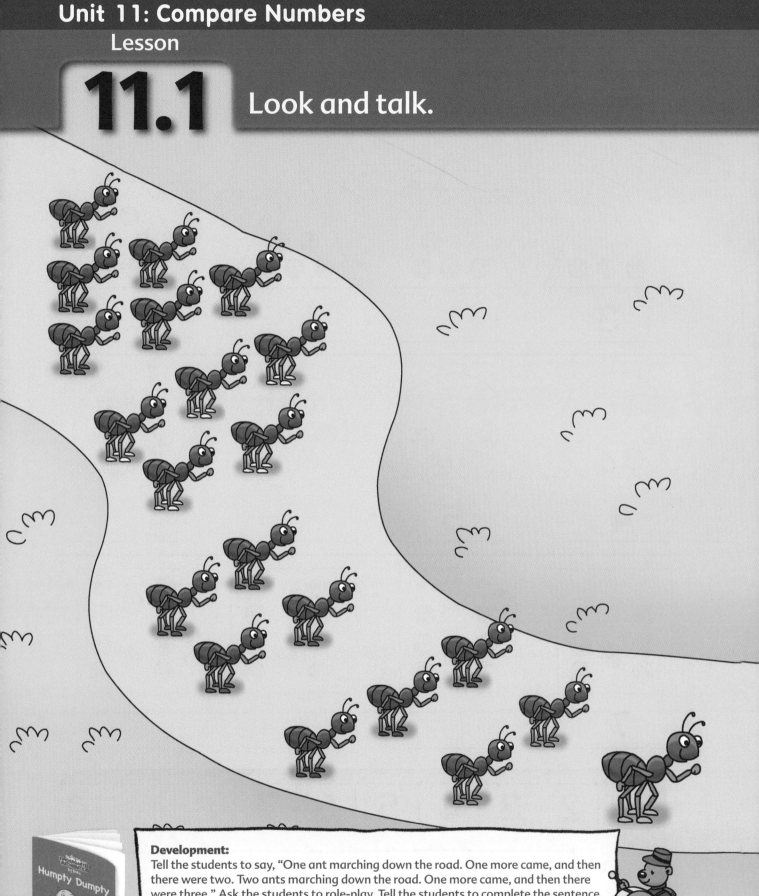

Development:
Tell the students to say, "One ant marching down the road. One more came, and then there were two. Two ants marching down the road. One more came, and then there were three." Ask the students to role-play. Tell the students to complete the sentence, "Six ants marching down the road. One more came, and then there were …"
Ask them to tell you the number of ants in each group and the number of ants in the group after that. Emphasize the idea of **one more**.

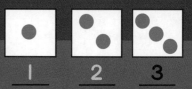

Fill in the missing numbers.

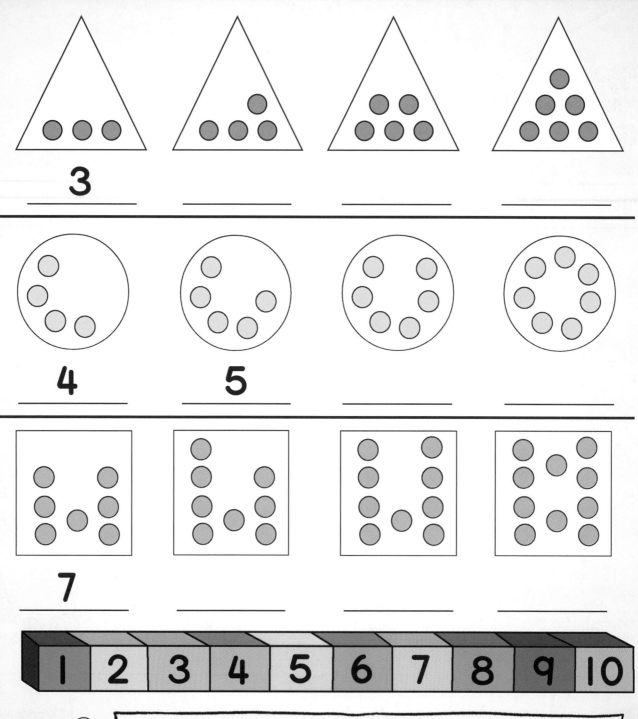

3 _____

4 _____   5 _____

7 _____

| 1 | 2 | 3 | 4 | 5 | 6 | 7 | 8 | 9 | 10 |

Development:
Tell the students to look at the first row of triangles on this page. Ask them, "What number is 1 more than 3?" Tell them to count the dots in the second triangle to confirm the answer. Repeat this with the next two sets. Ask the students to say, "4 is **1 more than** 3." while pointing to the numbers at the bottom of the page. Emphasize the idea of one more.

Development:
Give each student three small paper plates and some circular stickers. Ask the students to form a number pattern by pasting stickers on each plate. Explain that the number of stickers on the second plate should show a number that is **one less than** the first plate. Tell them to display their number patterns on the wall, starting with the greatest number. Ask the students to tell you the number of stickers on one plate and the number of stickers on the plate after it. Emphasize the idea of one less.

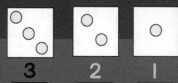
Fill in the missing numbers.

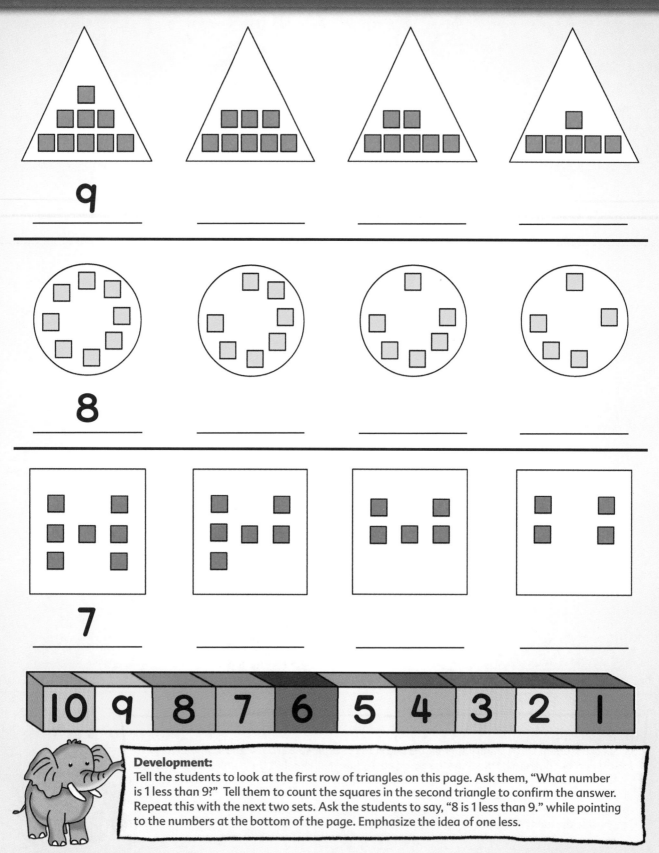

9

8

7

| 10 | 9 | 8 | 7 | 6 | 5 | 4 | 3 | 2 | 1 |

Development:
Tell the students to look at the first row of triangles on this page. Ask them, "What number is 1 less than 9?" Tell them to count the squares in the second triangle to confirm the answer. Repeat this with the next two sets. Ask the students to say, "8 is 1 less than 9." while pointing to the numbers at the bottom of the page. Emphasize the idea of one less.

11.3 Count and talk.

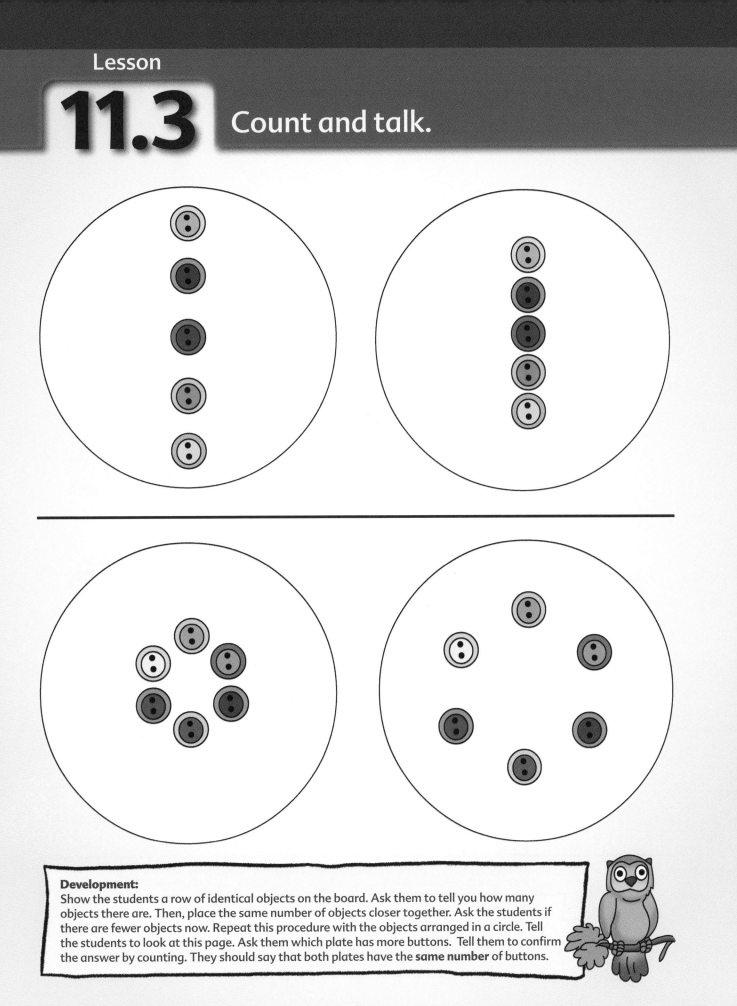

Development:
Show the students a row of identical objects on the board. Ask them to tell you how many objects there are. Then, place the same number of objects closer together. Ask the students if there are fewer objects now. Repeat this procedure with the objects arranged in a circle. Tell the students to look at this page. Ask them which plate has more buttons. Tell them to confirm the answer by counting. They should say that both plates have the **same number** of buttons.

Write the numbers.
Circle the set that has the same number.

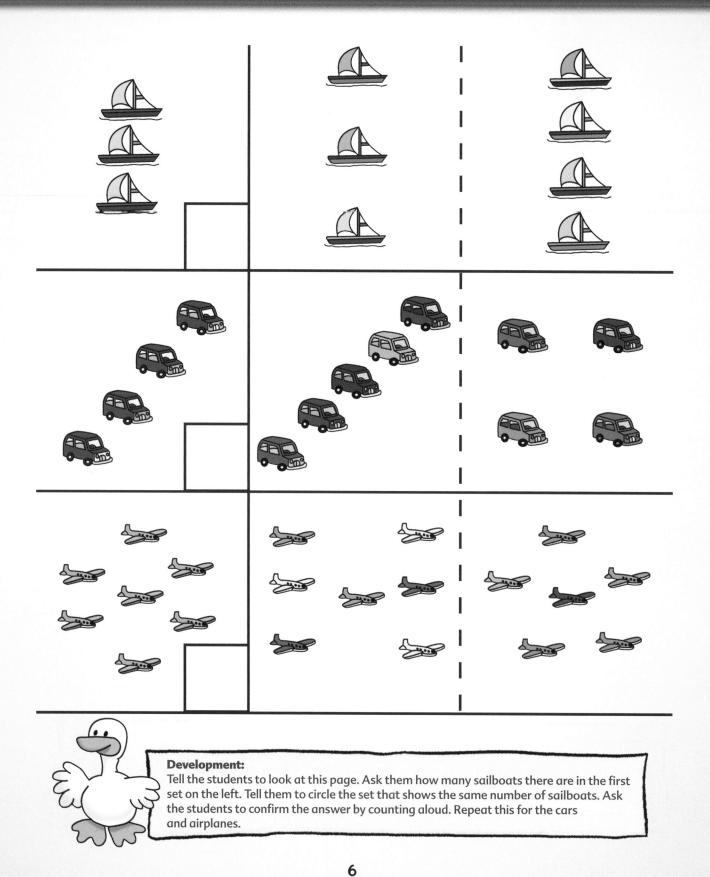

Development:
Tell the students to look at this page. Ask them how many sailboats there are in the first set on the left. Tell them to circle the set that shows the same number of sailboats. Ask the students to confirm the answer by counting aloud. Repeat this for the cars and airplanes.

Development:
Ask the students to do one-to-one matching. Tell them to draw imaginary lines using their fingers to match each knight to a horse. Then, have them tell you if there are more horses or knights by saying, "There is 1 more ... than ..." Repeat this by telling them to match each princess to a prince. The students should be able to say which set has one more.

Write the numbers.
Circle the set that has 1 more.

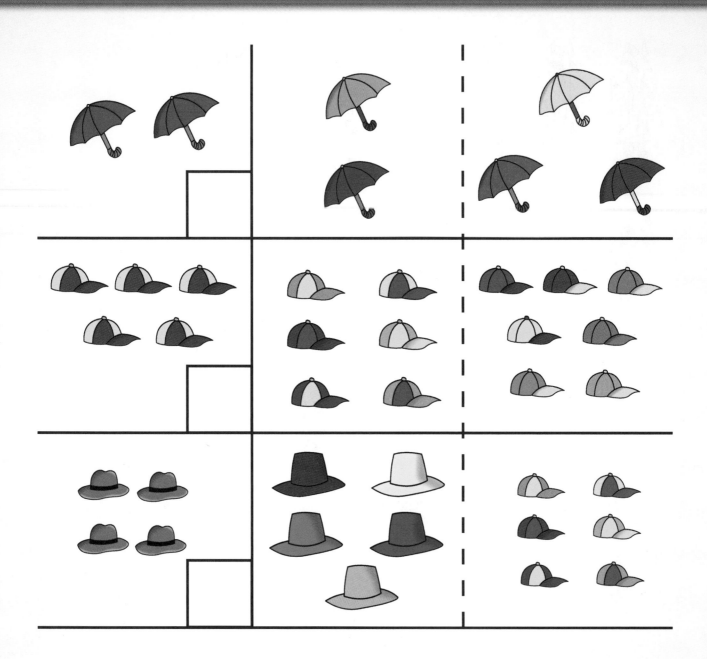

Development:
Ask two groups of students to come to the front of the classroom. There are four students in each group. Hold five pencils. Tell each student from one group to take a pencil from your hand. Place the additional pencil on the table. Ask the students to show the pencils they are holding. Then, hold up the additional pencil. Guide the students to say, "There are **fewer** children **than** pencils." Then, take another three different pencils. Ask each student from the other group to take a pencil from your hand. One student will not have a pencil. Tell the students to show the pencils they are holding. Encourage the students to say, "There are fewer pencils than children."

Write the numbers.
Circle the set that has 1 fewer.

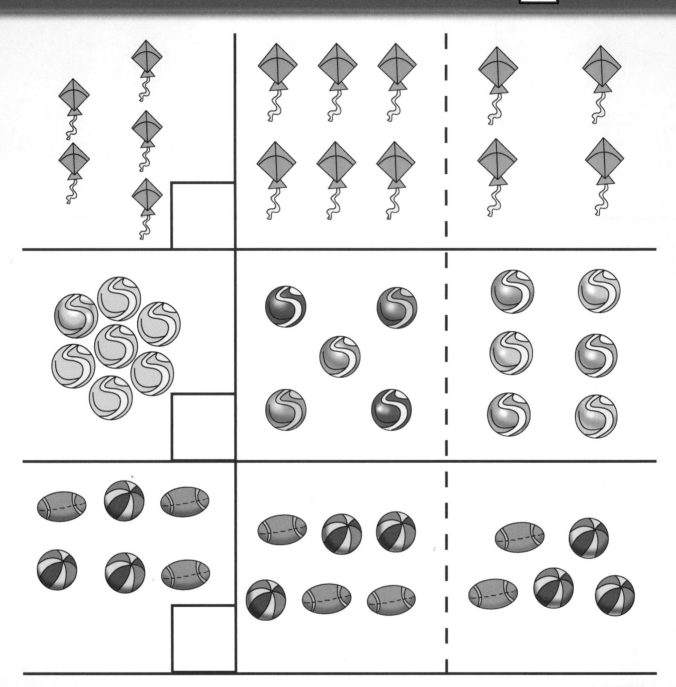

Development:
Show the students two sets of similar objects on the board, such that there is one more object in one of the sets. Ask the students to arrange the objects in two straight columns to do one-to-one matching. Ask them to tell which set has one object fewer. Tell the students to look at this page. Tell them to count the number of kites in the first set on the left. Then, ask them to circle the set that shows one kite fewer. Tell the students to confirm the answer by counting aloud.

Lesson
11.6
Draw lines to match.
Write the numbers.

○ is less than ○.

○ is less than ○.

Development:
Put up five flowers and three leaves on the board. Pair each flower with a leaf. Ask the students to count the number of flowers and leaves. Ask them, "Are there fewer flowers or leaves?" Guide them to say, "There are 5 flowers and 3 leaves. There are fewer leaves than flowers. 3 is less than 5." Repeat this by showing different numbers of flowers and leaves. Tell the students to look at this page. Ask them to count the number of flowers in each column. Tell them to draw lines to do one-to-one matching. Ask them to read each sentence "... is less than ..."

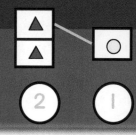

Draw lines to match.
Write the numbers.

(2) (1)

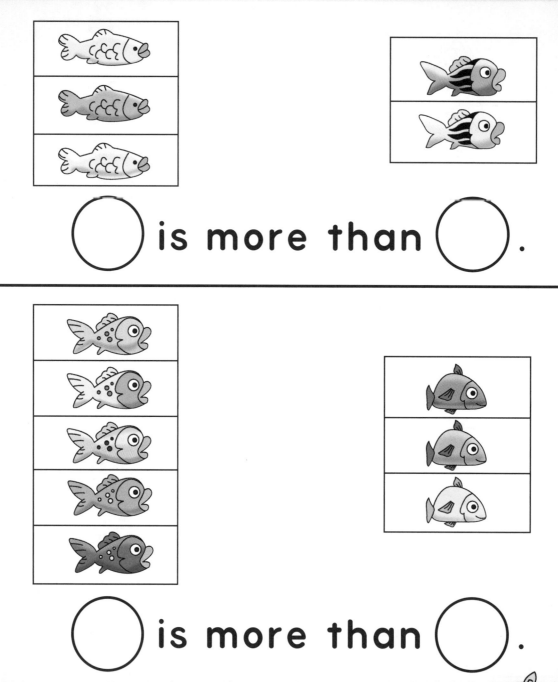

◯ is more than ◯.

◯ is more than ◯.

Development:
Put up six flowers and four leaves on the board. Pair each flower with a leaf. Ask the students to count the number of flowers and leaves. Ask them, "Are there more flowers or leaves?" Tell them to say, "There are 6 flowers and 4 leaves. There are more flowers than leaves. 6 is more than 4." Repeat this by showing different numbers of flowers and leaves. Ask the students to look at this page. Tell them to count the number of fish in each column. Tell them to draw lines to do one-to-one-matching. Ask them to read each sentence "... is more than ..."

Activity I, pages 2-4

11.7

Circle the correct word.
Write the numbers in the box.

3 is ☐ more than 2.
less

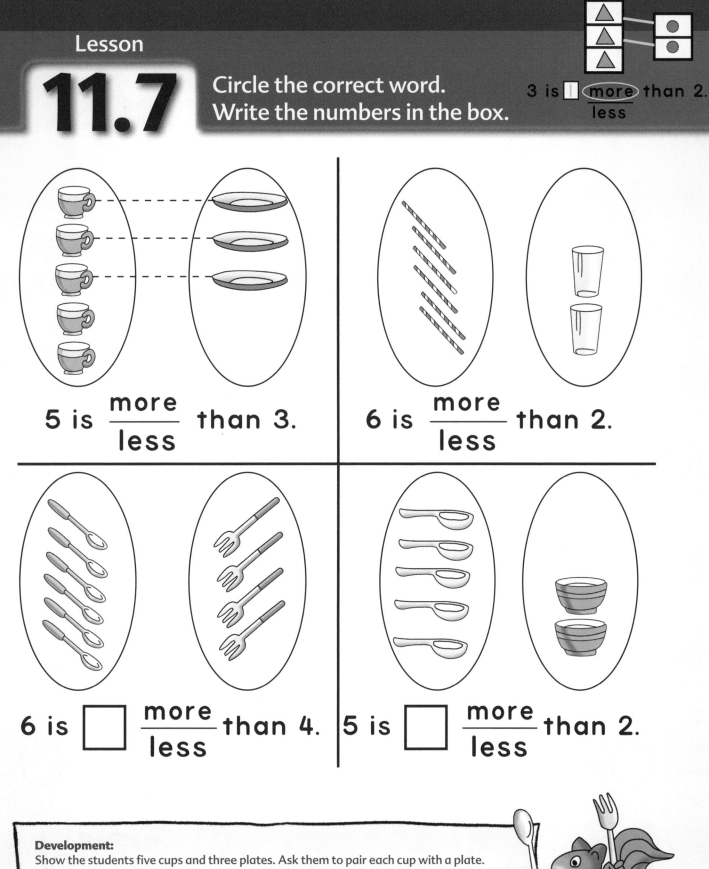

5 is $\dfrac{\text{more}}{\text{less}}$ than 3.

6 is $\dfrac{\text{more}}{\text{less}}$ than 2.

6 is ☐ $\dfrac{\text{more}}{\text{less}}$ than 4.

5 is ☐ $\dfrac{\text{more}}{\text{less}}$ than 2.

Development:
Show the students five cups and three plates. Ask them to pair each cup with a plate.
Then, tell them to count the number of cups and plates. Ask them, "Are there more cups
or plates?" Tell the students to say, "5 is more than 3." Next, ask them, "How many more?"
Lead them to say, "2 more." Draw the students' attention to this page. Ask them to draw
lines to do one-to-one matching. Then, tell them to say, "... is more than ..." Ask them,
"How many more?" Finally, guide them to say, "5 is more than 3. 5 is 2 more than 3."

Draw lines to match.
Write the numbers.

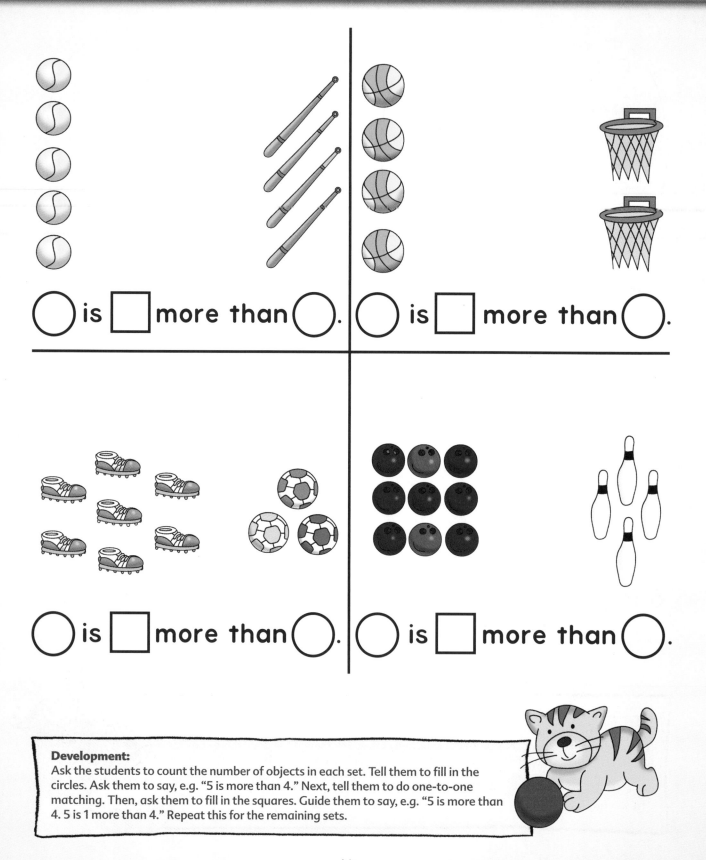

○ is ☐ more than ○. ○ is ☐ more than ○.

○ is ☐ more than ○. ○ is ☐ more than ○.

Development:
Ask the students to count the number of objects in each set. Tell them to fill in the circles. Ask them to say, e.g. "5 is more than 4." Next, tell them to do one-to-one matching. Then, ask them to fill in the squares. Guide them to say, e.g. "5 is more than 4. 5 is 1 more than 4." Repeat this for the remaining sets.

14
fourteen

11.8

Circle the correct word.
Write the numbers in the box.

I is ☐ more / less than 2.

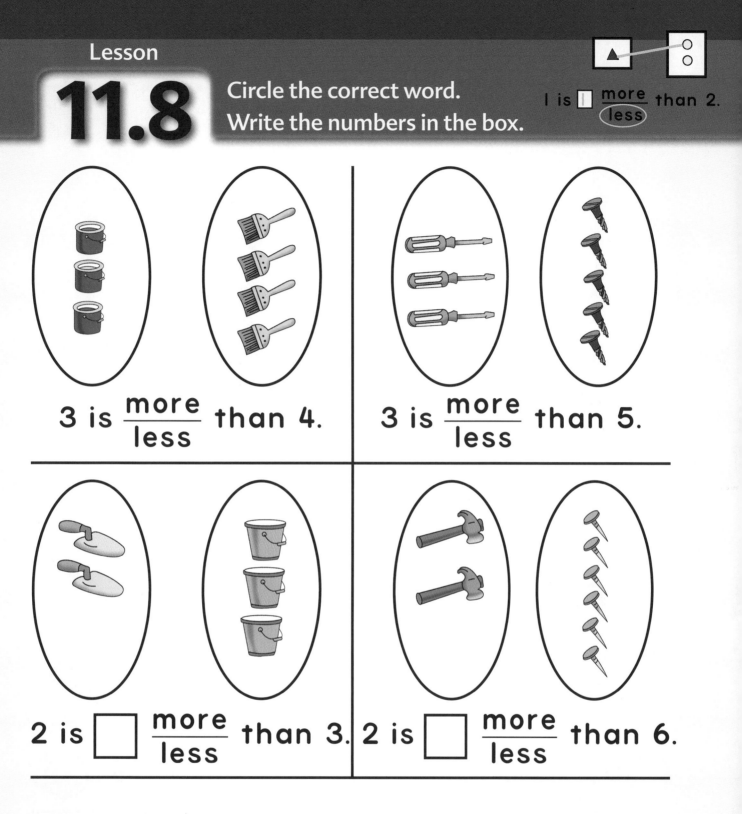

3 is more / less than 4.

3 is more / less than 5.

2 is ☐ more / less than 3.

2 is ☐ more / less than 6.

Development:
Show the students three small pots of paint and four paintbrushes. Ask them to pair each pot with a paintbrush. Then, tell them to count the number of pots and paintbrushes. Ask them, "Are there more pots or paintbrushes?" Ask the students to say, "3 is less than 4." Next, ask them, "How many less?" Lead them to say, "1 less." Draw the students' attention to this page. Ask them to draw lines to do one-to-one matching. Then, tell them to say, "... is less than ..." Ask them, "How many less?" Finally, ask them to say, "3 is less than 4. 3 is 1 less than 4."

Draw lines to match.
Write the numbers.

1 is ☐ less than 2.

○ is ☐ less than ○.

○ is ☐ less than ○.

○ is ☐ less than ○.

○ is ☐ less than ○.

Development:
Ask the students to count the number of items in each set. Tell them to fill in the circles. Ask them to say, "2 is less than 3." Next, tell them to do one-to-one matching. Then, ask them to fill in the squares. Guide them to say, "2 is less than 3. 2 is 1 less than 3."

Activities 3 to 5, pages 8-17

Draw a set that has 1 more.

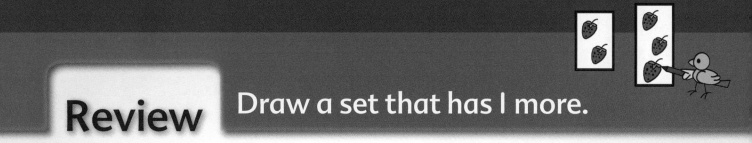

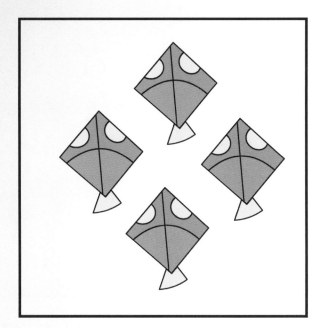

Draw a set that has 1 less.

Count.
Write the numbers.

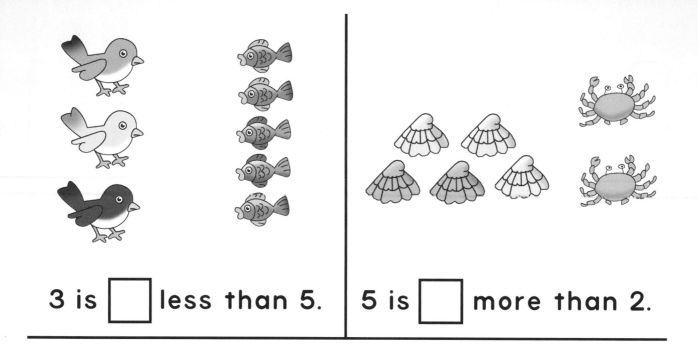

3 is ☐ less than 5.

5 is ☐ more than 2.

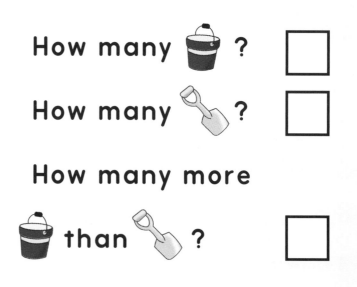

How many 🪣 ? ☐

How many 🥄 ? ☐

How many more

🪣 than 🥄 ? ☐

12.1 Look and talk.

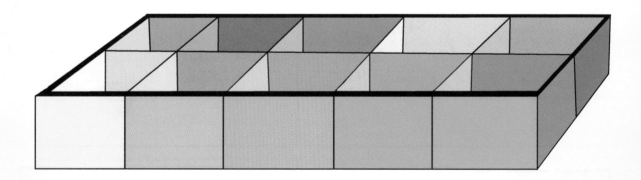

Development:
Give each pair of students 14 small objects and a container with ten slots, e.g. an egg carton with ten cups. Ask the students to guess if there are enough slots for the given objects. Say, "Do you think there are enough slots for these things?" Have them check their responses by putting one object in each slot. Repeat this with 9 and 12 objects. Tell the students to look at this page. Ask them to guess if there are enough slots to keep the toy animals by putting one toy in each slot. Have them check their responses by pointing at a toy and a slot at the same time with their left and right hand respectively.

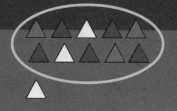

Count and circle 10 things.

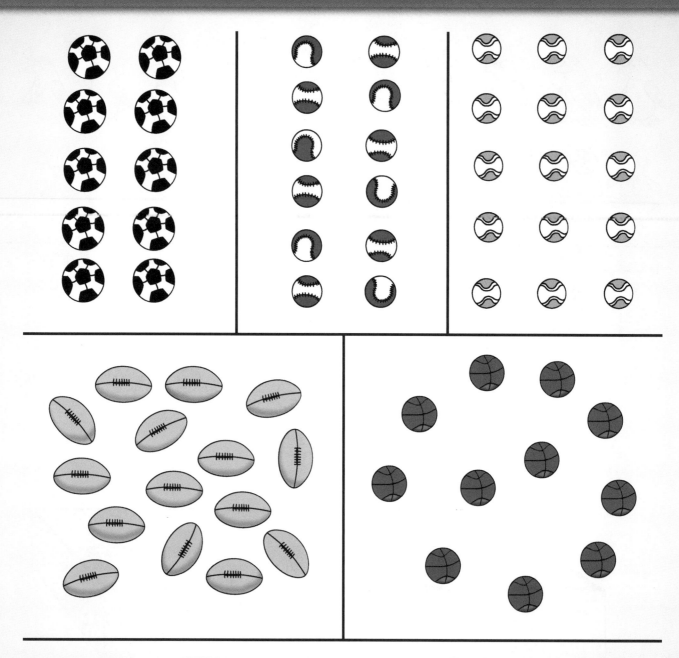

Development:
Place 13 objects in a cluster on the board. Draw a table with two rows and five columns on the board. Ask the students, "Do you think there are enough boxes to keep all these things if we put one thing in each box?" Have the students move ten objects into the table by placing one object in each box to check their responses. Repeat this with 8 and 11 objects. Next, replace the two by five table with a circle. Show the students 15 objects. Ask the students, "Do you think there are more or fewer than ten things here?" Have the students move ten objects into the circle to check their responses. Tell the students to look at this page. Each time, ask, "Do you think there are more or fewer than ten soccer balls here?" Ask the students to count ten soccer balls and to circle them. Then, tell the students to count aloud to confirm the number of balls in the circle. Finally, guide the students to say, "Ten balls and a few more."

12.2

Circle 10 things.
Write the numbers.

10 and 1

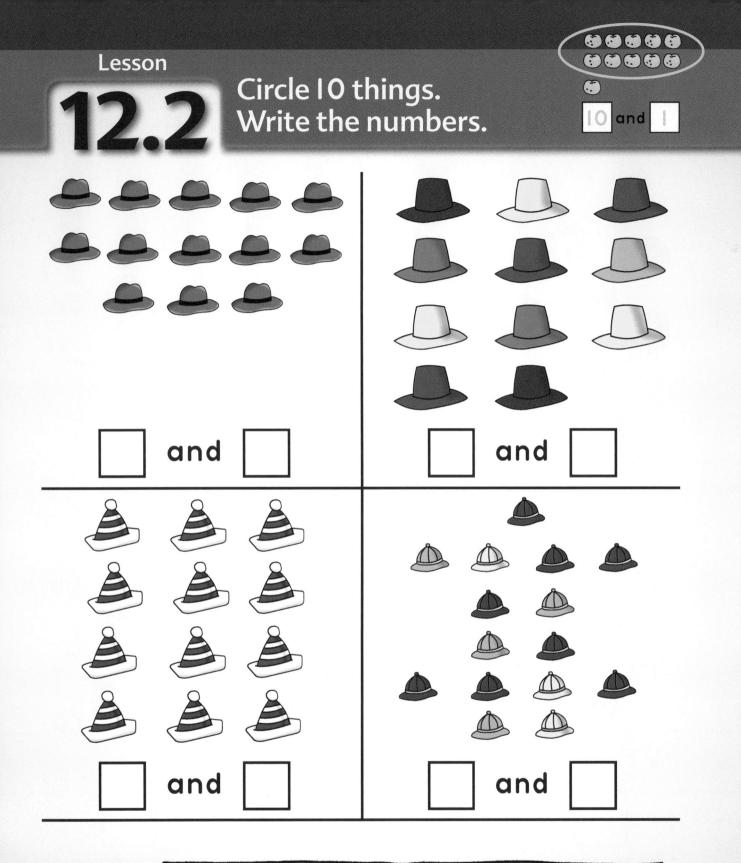

☐ and ☐

☐ and ☐

☐ and ☐

☐ and ☐

Development:
Place 14 objects on the board in a cluster. Ask a student to arrange these in rows. Tell another student to move ten objects apart from the others. Point to each group of objects and ask, "How many things are there in this group?" Lead the students to say, " 10 and 4 ." Repeat with different numbers of objects. Ask the students to look at this page. Tell the students to circle ten hats in each set. Then, ask the class to say, " 10 and ..." before writing the correct numbers.

Circle 10 things.
Write the numbers.

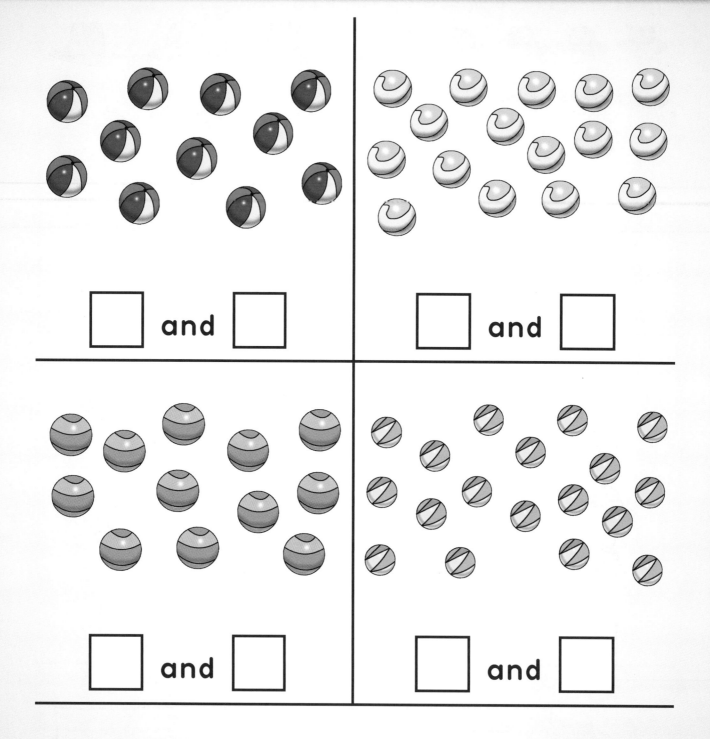

10 and 3

☐ and ☐

☐ and ☐

☐ and ☐

☐ and ☐

Consolidation:
Ask the students to circle ten balls. Then, ask them to say, " 10 and ..." before writing the correct numbers.

Activity 1, pages 18-19

Count.
Write the numbers.

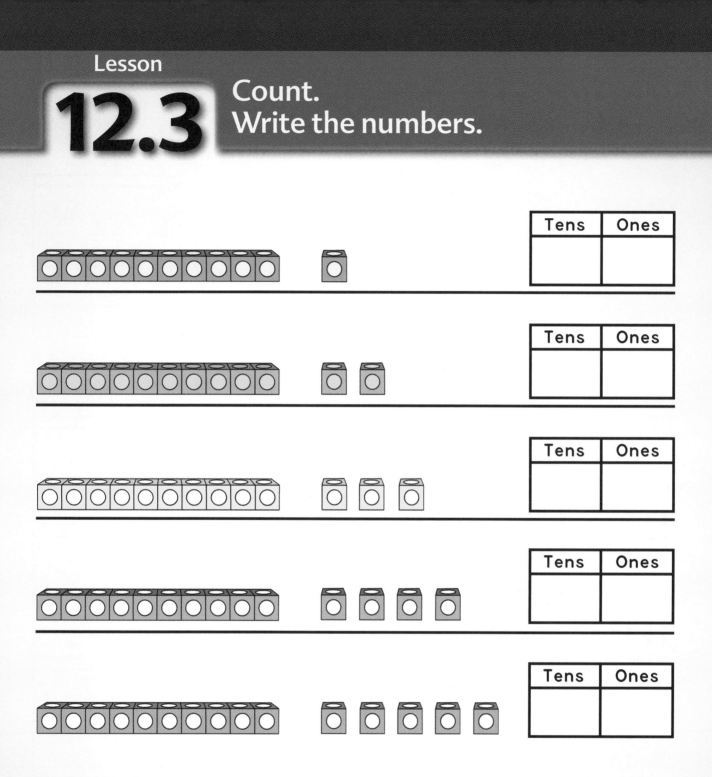

Tens	Ones

Tens	Ones

Tens	Ones

Tens	Ones

Tens	Ones

Development:
Give each student 13 connect-a-cubes. Ask them to join ten cubes together. Ask them to hold up the connected cubes and say, "Ten." Tell them to count the cubes that are not connected and say, "Three." Then, tell them to say, " 10 and 3 ." Repeat this with 11 and 16 cubes. Ask them to look at this page. Give each student 11 connect-a-cubes. Tell them to join ten cubes together. Ask them to hold up the connected cubes and say, "This is 1 ten." Ask them, "How many **tens** are there?" Check that they say, "1 ten." Then ask, "How many **ones** are there?" Show them how to fill in the boxes on the page. Repeat this for numbers 12 to 15, each time giving the students one more cube to make up the correct number.

Circle 10 things.
Write the numbers.

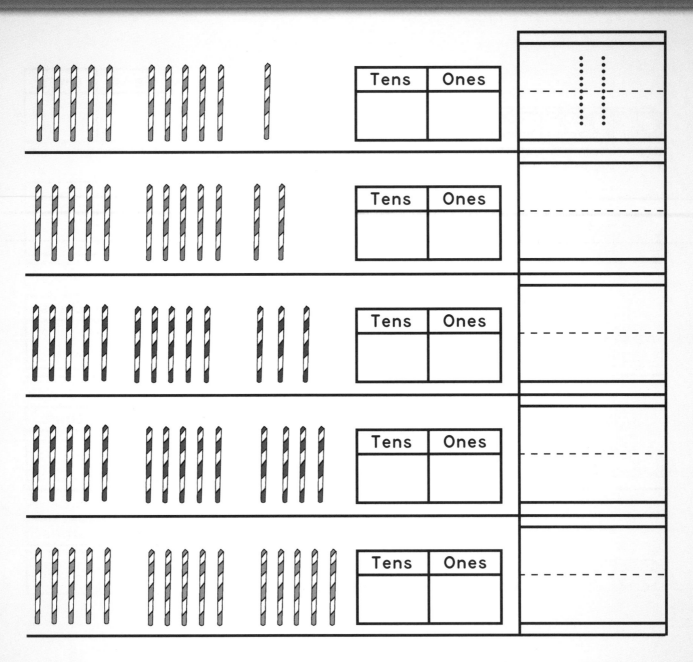

Tens	Ones

Tens	Ones

Tens	Ones

Tens	Ones

Tens	Ones

Development:
Give each student 11 straws and some string. Tell the students to tie ten straws together. Ask them, "How many tens are there? How many ones are there?" Then, show them how to fill in the boxes on this page by pasting cards with the digits 1 and 1 on the board. Then, move these cards to show them the same number written as 11. Say, "This is 11. 11 is 1 ten and 1 one." Tell the students to look at this page. Ask them to count ten straws and to circle them. Ask them, "How many tens are there? How many ones are there?" Tell them to fill in the boxes and to write the numeral 11, while saying, "Eleven." Repeat this for numbers 12 to 15.

12.4

Count.
Write the numbers.

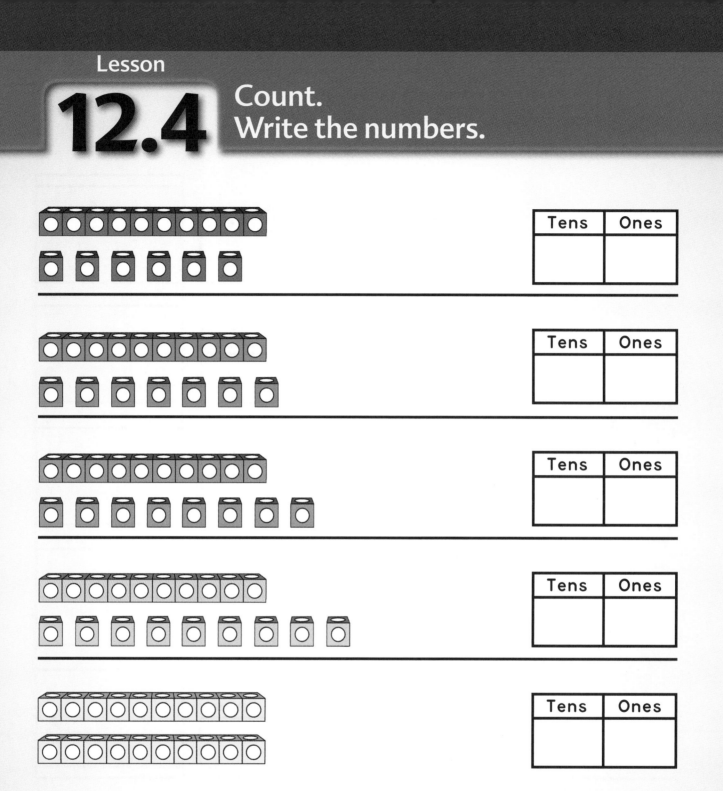

Tens	Ones

Tens	Ones

Tens	Ones

Tens	Ones

Tens	Ones

Development:
Give each student 17 connect-a-cubes. Ask them to join ten cubes together. Ask them to hold up the connected cubes and say, "Ten." Tell them to count the cubes that are not connected and say, "Seven." Ask them to say, "10 and 7." Repeat this with 15 and 19 cubes.
Give each student 16 connect-a-cubes. Ask them to join ten cubes together. Ask them to hold up the connected cubes and say, "This is 1 ten." Ask them, "How many tens are there?" Check that they say, "1 ten." Then ask, "How many ones are there?" Show them how to fill in the boxes on the page. Repeat this for numbers 17 to 20, each time giving the students one more cube to make up the correct number.

Circle 10 things.
Write the numbers.

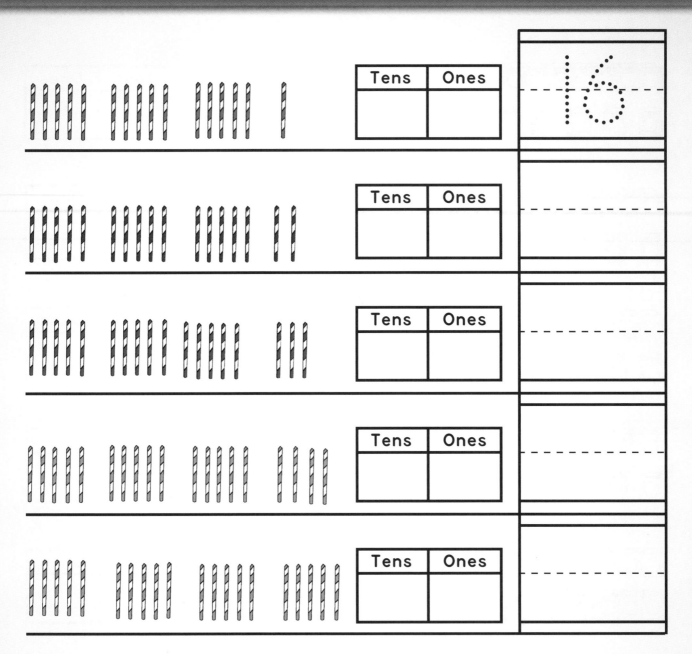

Tens	Ones

16

Tens	Ones

Tens	Ones

Tens	Ones

Tens	Ones

Development:
Give each student 16 straws and some string. Tell them to tie ten straws together. Ask them, "How many tens are there? How many ones are there?" Then, show them how to fill in the boxes on this page by putting up the digits 1 and 6 on the board. Then, move these cards to show them the same number written as 16. Say, "This is 16. 16 is 1 ten and 6 ones."
Tell the students to look at this page. Ask the students to count ten straws and to circle them. Ask them, "How many tens are there? How many ones are there?" Tell them to fill in the boxes and to write the numeral 16, while saying, "Sixteen." Repeat this for numbers 17 to 20.

Activities 2 and 3, pages 20-24

Lesson

12.5

Color 10 shapes blue.
Color more shapes
red to make the correct number.

11	
Tens	Ones
I	I

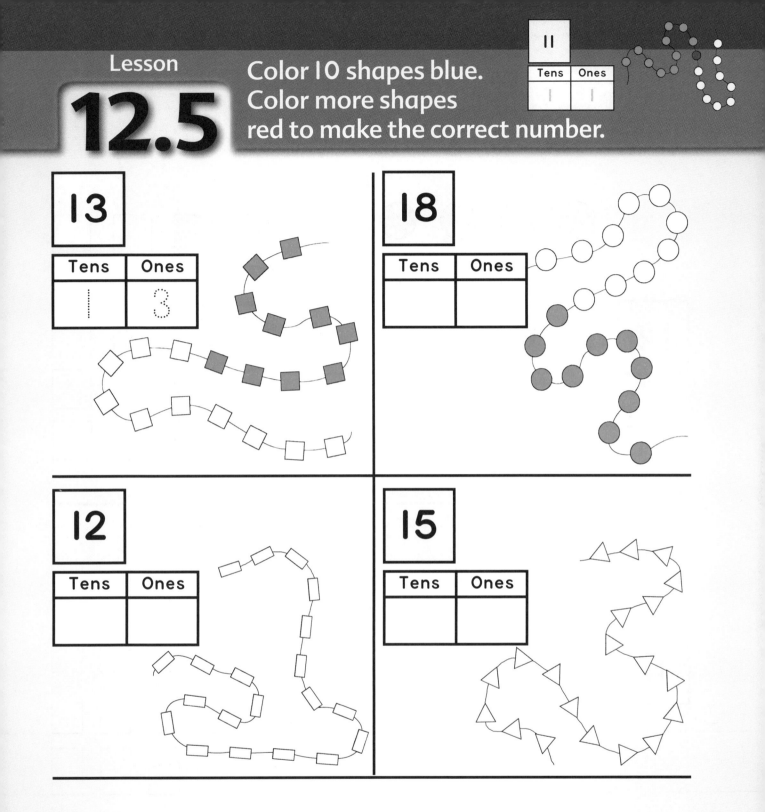

13	
Tens	**Ones**
I	3

18	
Tens	**Ones**

12	
Tens	**Ones**

15	
Tens	**Ones**

Development:
Show the numeral 17 by putting up the numeral cards for 1 and 7 on the board. Next to this, draw a **place value chart**, similar to the one on this page. Show the students one string of beads and say, "1 ten." Show them another seven sticks and say, "7 ones." Say, "17 is 1 ten and 7 ones." Repeat this with 12, 15 and 18. Ask the students to look at this page. Read the number, "13" to the students. Ask them, "How many tens are there? How many ones?" Tell them to write the numeral 13 in the boxes. Ask them to count the blue squares and color three more squares red. Emphasize that there is 1 ten as you point to the blue squares, and 3 ones as you point to the red squares.

Color 10 shapes blue. Color more shapes red to make the correct number.

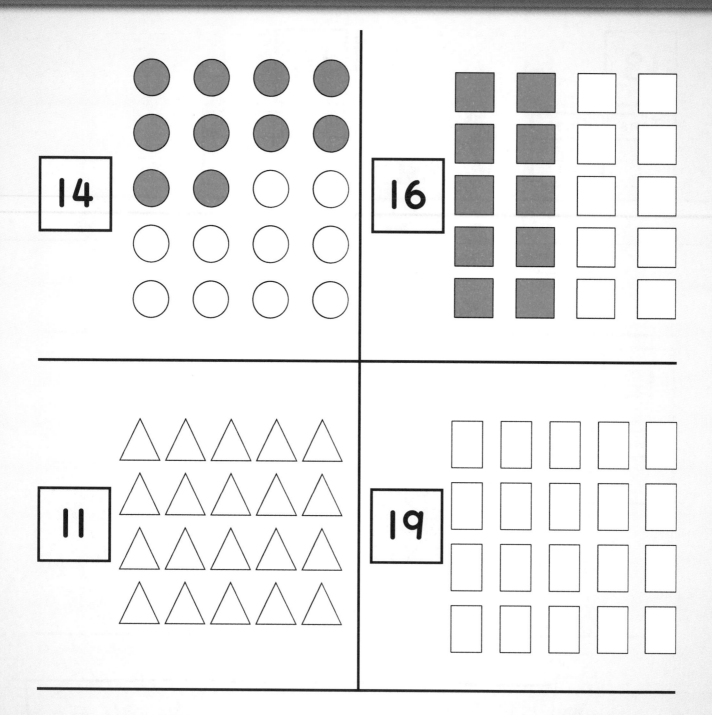

14

16

11

19

Consolidation:
Read each number to the students. For each number, ask, "How many tens are there? How many ones?" Ask them to color ten shapes blue and the correct number of shapes red to make up each number. Tell them to look at the colored shapes and say, e.g. "14 is 1 ten and 4 ones."

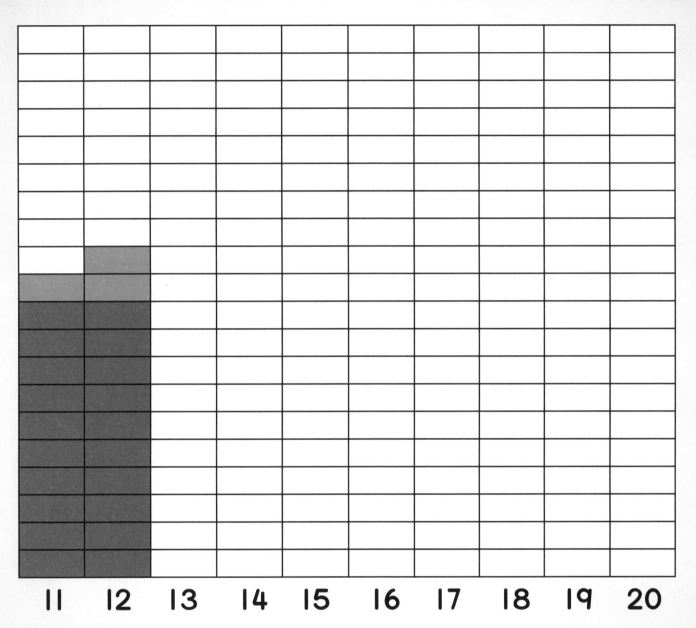

| 11 | 12 | 13 | 14 | 15 | 16 | 17 | 18 | 19 | 20 |

Development:
Give each student a set of ten cubes connected in a column. Tell them to hold up one more cube and say, "11." Guide them to say, "1 more than 10 is 11." Continue in this way for numbers 12 to 20. Ask the students to look at this page. Ask them to say, "11 is 10 and 1." Then, get them to say, "1 more than 11 is 12. 12 is 10 and 2." Continue in this way for numbers 13 to 20.

Fill in the missing numbers.

Socks on the line: 11 12 ___ 14 ___ 16 17 ___ 19 20

Mice: 20 17 14 13 11

Development:
Ask the students to say the numbers one to ten in order. Then, ask them to say the numbers 11 to 20 in order. Tell a student to pick a numeral card and to read the number aloud. Tell the class to say the numbers that follow up to 20. Repeat this with different volunteers. Ask another student to hold a ball. This student says any number from 11 to 19 and passes the ball to another student. The student who receives the ball continues by saying the number that comes next. When the students have arrived at 20, get them to play the game again by saying the numbers in reverse order. Ask the students to look at this page. Ask them to say each number aloud as they point to the sock/mouse. Then, tell them to write the missing numbers. After the students have completed the exercise, say the numbers to them, e.g. "11." Tell the class to respond by saying, e.g. "11 is 10 and 1."

Activities 4 and 5. pages 25-27

Count.
Write the numbers.

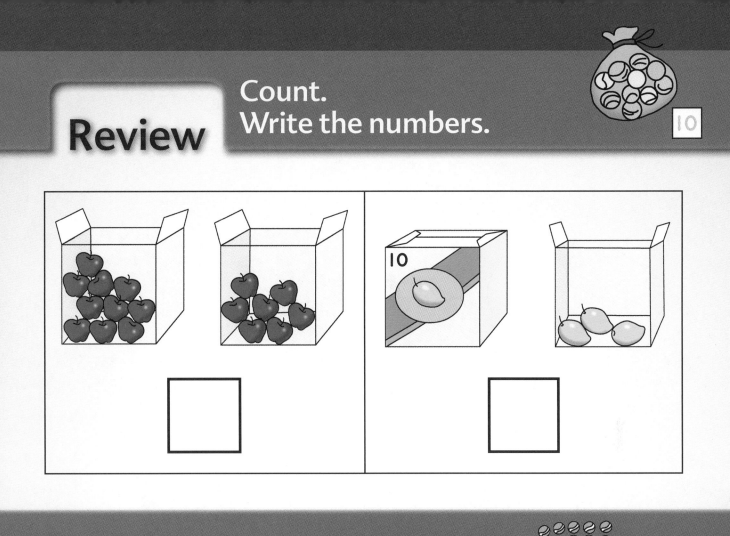

Draw more to show the correct number.

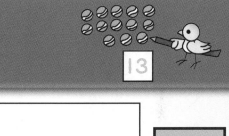

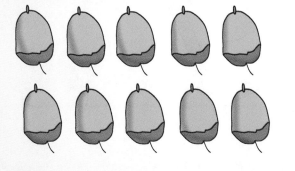

16

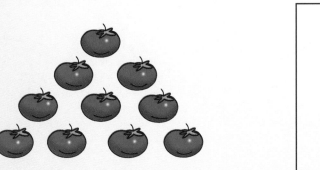

19

Fill in the missing numbers.

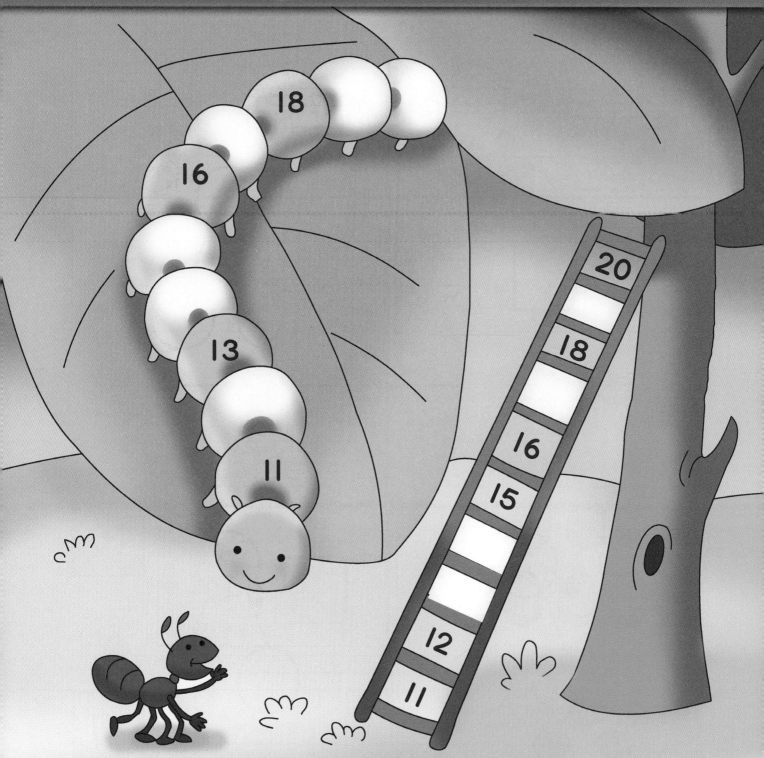

Development:
Tell the students to look at the ducks on this page. Ask the students, "How many ducks are in the water?" Then ask, "How many ducks are not in the water?" Finally, ask, "How many ducks are there **altogether**?" Repeat this with the dogs and birds.

Count.
Write the numbers.

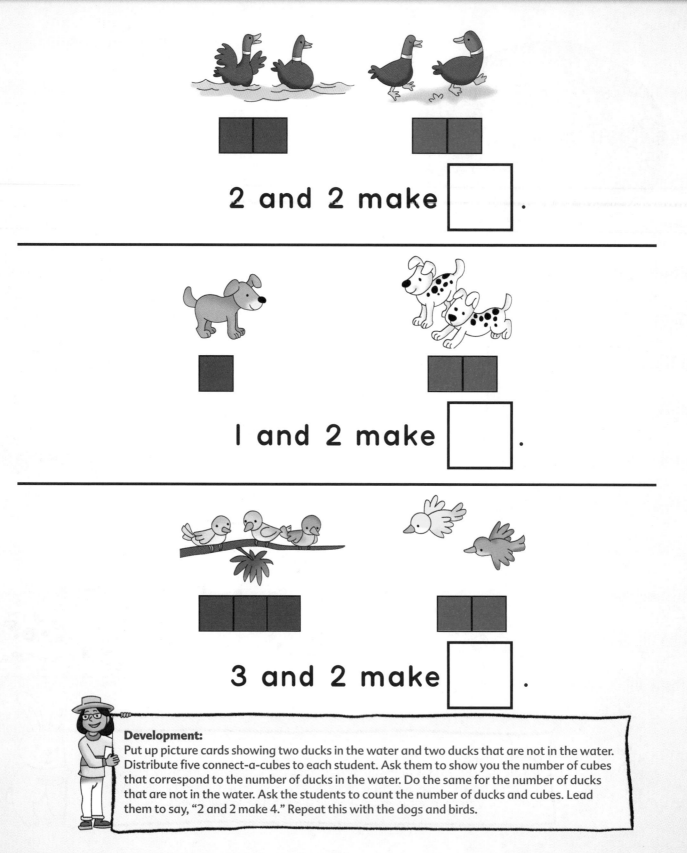

2 and 2 make ☐.

1 and 2 make ☐.

3 and 2 make ☐.

Development:
Put up picture cards showing two ducks in the water and two ducks that are not in the water. Distribute five connect-a-cubes to each student. Ask them to show you the number of cubes that correspond to the number of ducks in the water. Do the same for the number of ducks that are not in the water. Ask the students to count the number of ducks and cubes. Lead them to say, "2 and 2 make 4." Repeat this with the dogs and birds.

13.2 Look and talk.

Development:
Have the students look at this page. Tell the students to sort the children according to gender and color of the children's clothes. Ask the students, "How many boys are there? How many girls are there?" Finally, ask, "How many children are there altogether?" Repeat this with the color of the children's clothes and the flowers.

Count.
Write the numbers.

1 and 2 make **3**.

2 and 3 make ☐.

1 and 4 make ☐.

☐ and ☐ make ☐.

☐ and ☐ make ☐.

Activity 1. pages 28-30

13.3 Look and talk.

Count.
Write the numbers.

Development:
Ask the students to count the hens and roosters on this page. Tell them to write the number of hens, followed by the number of roosters in the first number bond. Next, tell them to write the number of roosters, followed by the number of hens in the second number bond. Finally, guide the students in obtaining the total number of chickens with the help of connect-a-cubes. Encourage the class to say, "... and ... make ..." Repeat this with the different colored ducks.

Activity 2. pages 31-33

13.4 Look, do and talk.

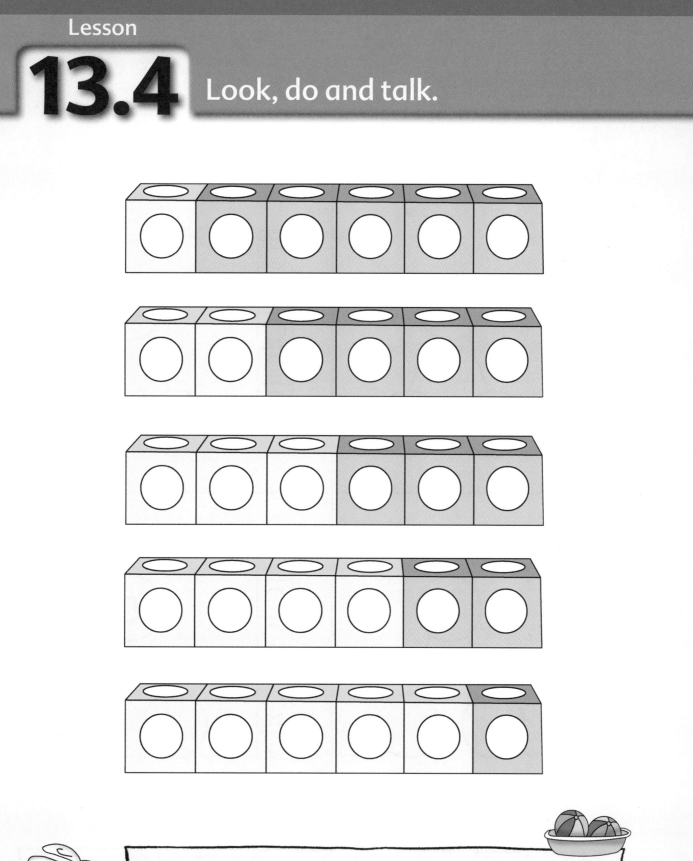

Development:
Give each student ten connect-a-cubes: five in one color, another five in a different color. Instruct the students to form the first row of cubes shown on this page. Then, tell them to remove the cube that is in a different color from the rest in the row. Finally, ask them to say, "... and ... make 6." Repeat this for the remaining rows of cubes on this page.

Color the  to show different ways to make 6.
Write the numbers.

Development:
Give each student six connect-a-cubes joined in a row. Ask the students to break the row of six cubes into two parts in different ways. Instruct the students to color the cubes on this page using two different colors to show the two parts they have formed. Guide the students as they complete the number bonds on this page.

Activity 3, pages 34-36

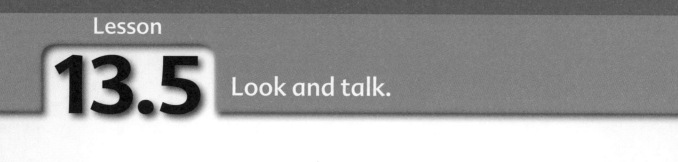

Development:
Put up a picture of seven dolls on the board. Ask the students to sort the dolls into two groups in any way they wish. Each time, tell the students to say, "... and ... make 7." Tell the students to look at this page. Ask them to tell you how the dolls on this page have been grouped. Encourage them to group the seven dolls in other ways. Accept all reasonable responses. Tell them to count the number of dolls in each group and to say, "... and ... make 7."

Color the  to show different ways to make 7. Write the numbers.

6
2   4

7

7

7

7

Development:
Give each student seven connect-a-cubes joined in a row. Tell the students to break the row of seven cubes into two parts in different ways. Instruct the students to color the cubes on this page using two different colors to show the two parts they have formed. Guide the students as they complete the number bonds on this page.

13.6 Do and talk.

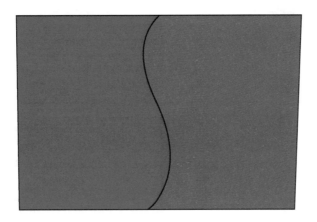

Development:
Set up a game mat in the middle of the room. Form teams of two students. Give each student four small beanbags. One team stands on the blue side of the mat, the other stands on the red side of the mat. Students on the blue side have to throw their beanbags onto the red side of the mat, and vice versa. Have the students take turns to throw a beanbag at a time. After all students have thrown their beanbags, ask them to count the beanbags on each side of the mat and say, "... and ... make ..."

Count.
Write the numbers.

Development:
Ask the students to count the number of red and blue dots shown in each question. Show the students how to record their answers in the number bonds. Finally, ask the class to say, "... and ... make 8."

13.7

Do and count.
Write the numbers.

Development:
Give each student pieces of paper each with nine identical circles arranged as shown on this page. Ask the students to cut each piece into two parts containing a number of circles. Encourage them to do this in different ways. Tell them to show the class how they have done it. Ask the students to count the number of circles in each part. Ask them to say, "... and ... make 9." Show them how to complete the number bonds on this page.

Do and count.
Write the numbers.

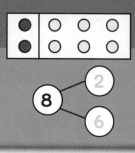

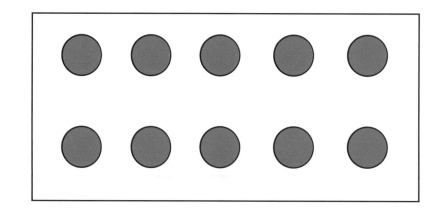

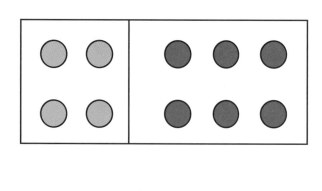

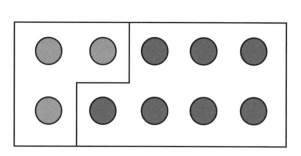

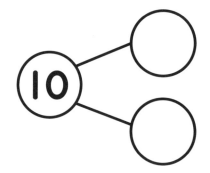

Development:
Give each student pieces of paper each with ten identical circles arranged as shown on this page. Ask the students to cut each piece into two parts containing a number of circles. Encourage them to do this in different ways. Tell them to show the class how they have done it. Ask the students to count the number of circles in each part. Ask them to say, "... and ... make 10." Show them how to complete the number bonds on this page.

46
forty-six

Activities 4 and 5, pages 37-39

Count.
Write the numbers.

2 and 1 make 3.

4 and 2 make ☐.

3 and 5 make ☐.

☐ and ☐ make ☐.

Color the ⬚ using two colors.
Write the numbers.

14.1   Look and talk.

Development:
Show the class picture cards of two birds on a bird stand and three birds on a branch, or get the students to act out the situation. Tell the students to talk about where the birds are. Ask the class, "How many birds are there on the bird stand? How many birds are there on the branch?" Then, ask, "How many birds are there **altogether**?" Tell them to count the birds on this page. Repeat this with the dogs and cats.

Add.
Write the numbers.

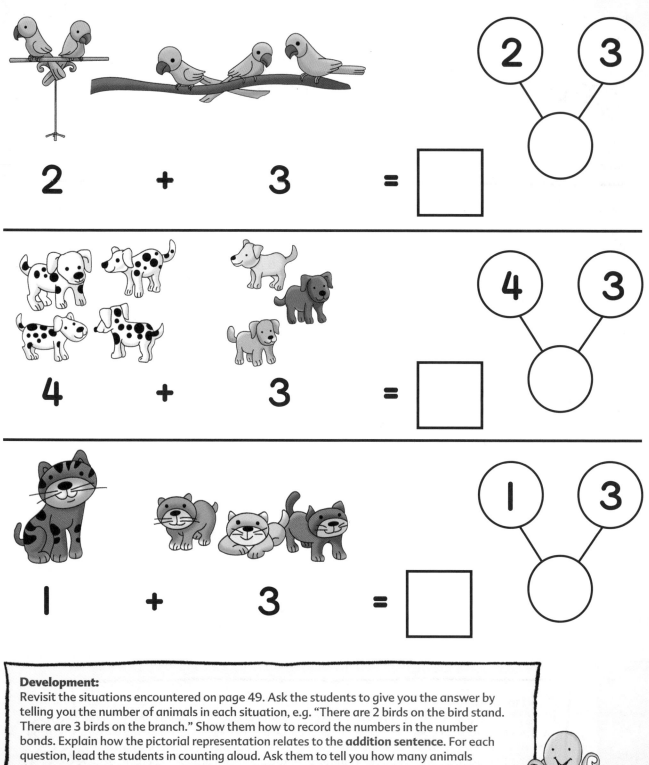

2 + 2 = 4

2   +   3   =   ☐

4   +   3   =   ☐

1   +   3   =   ☐

Development:
Revisit the situations encountered on page 49. Ask the students to give you the answer by telling you the number of animals in each situation, e.g. "There are 2 birds on the bird stand. There are 3 birds on the branch." Show them how to record the numbers in the number bonds. Explain how the pictorial representation relates to the **addition sentence**. For each question, lead the students in counting aloud. Ask them to tell you how many animals there are altogether. Finally, say, "There are 2 birds on the bird stand. There are 3 birds on a branch. There are 5 birds altogether." Point to 2, +, 3, = and 5 as you do so.

Activity I. pages 40–42

14.2

Add.
Write the numbers.

③ ②
⑤
3 + 2 = 5
●●● ▪▪

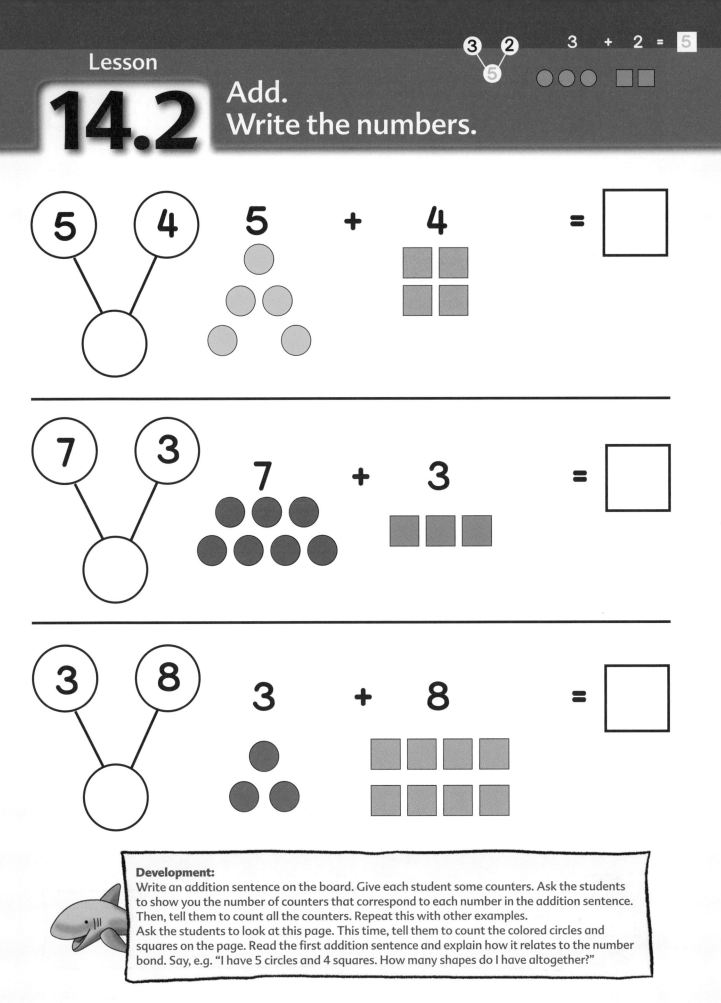

5   4

5   +   4   =   ☐

7   3

7   +   3   =   ☐

3   8

3   +   8   =   ☐

Development:
Write an addition sentence on the board. Give each student some counters. Ask the students to show you the number of counters that correspond to each number in the addition sentence. Then, tell them to count all the counters. Repeat this with other examples.
Ask the students to look at this page. This time, tell them to count the colored circles and squares on the page. Read the first addition sentence and explain how it relates to the number bond. Say, e.g. "I have 5 circles and 4 squares. How many shapes do I have altogether?"

Color the correct number of ■ and ●.
Write the numbers.

3 + 3 = 6

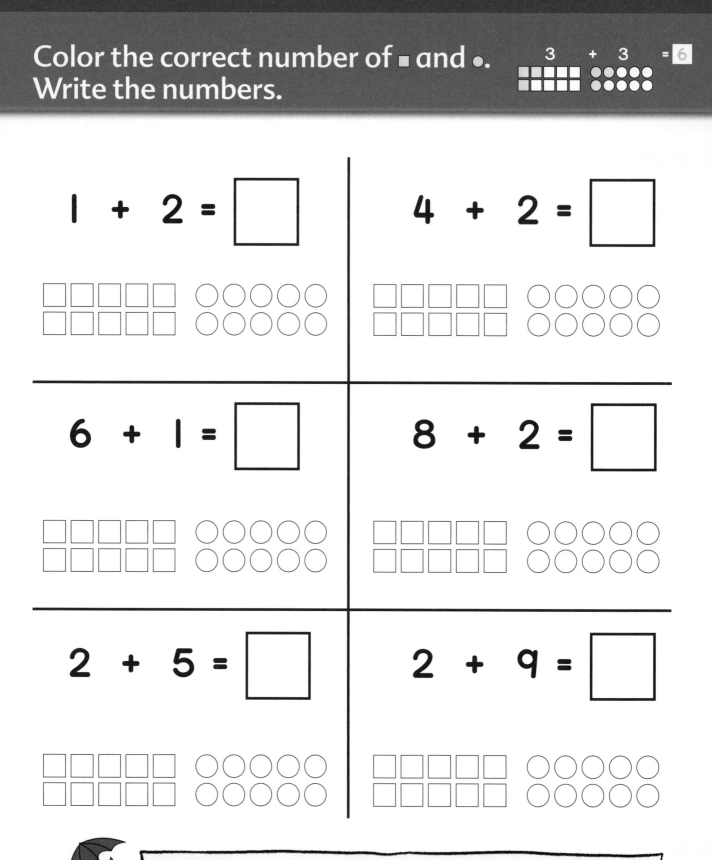

1 + 2 = ▢

4 + 2 = ▢

6 + 1 = ▢

8 + 2 = ▢

2 + 5 = ▢

2 + 9 = ▢

Development:
Ask the students to read each addition sentence aloud. Tell them to color the correct number of squares and circles. Then, ask them to count the total number of colored shapes. Each time, ask the class, "Is the answer more than 10?"

Activity 2. pages 43-44

14.3 Look and talk.

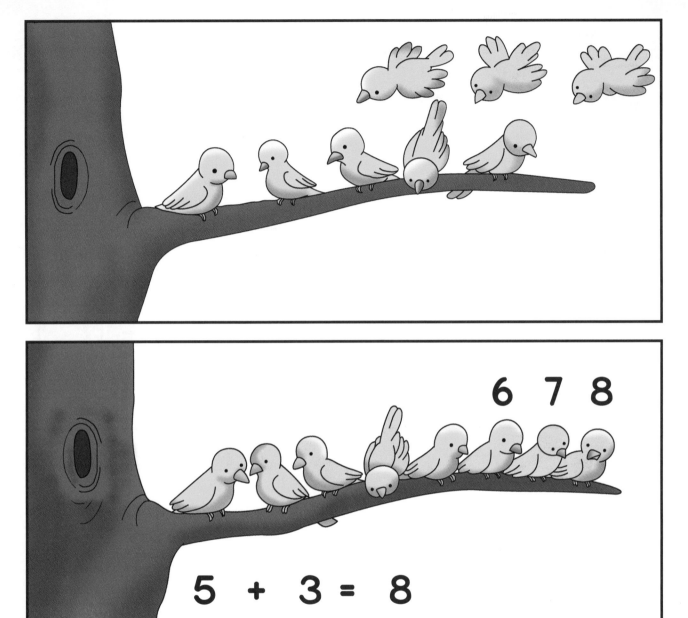

$$5 + 3 = 8$$

Introduction:
Tell the class a story about five birds sitting on a branch.

Development:
Use pictures of birds as you do so, or ask the students to act out the situation. Tell them to count and confirm the number of birds. Then, show three birds joining these five birds. Ask, "How many birds were there on the branch at first? Can you remember without counting again?" Then, ask the students to count on by pointing at the birds that have just joined the rest. Retell the story as you show the students the number sentence on this page. Say, "There were 5 birds. Then, 3 birds joined them. How many birds are there altogether?" Lead the class to count on, "5, 6, 7, 8".

Add.
Write the numbers.

$$7 + 2 = \boxed{}$$

$$6 + 5 = \boxed{}$$

$$3 + 9 = \boxed{}$$

Development:
Ask seven students to come to the front of the class. Tell the class to count the number of students in this group. Ask the seven students to count and confirm their classmates' answer. Then, invite two more children to join the group of seven. Tell the class to count on as this happens. Point to the group of students and ask the class, "How many students are there now?" Ask the students to look at this page. Tell them to count the number of ants already at the cake. Get the students to write down the number. Then, ask them to count on to include the ants that are joining the rest. Relate the addition sentence to the picture. Repeat this with the bees and mice.

Activity 3, pages 45-47

6 + 3

6 + 4

7 + 5

Development:
Put up six squares on the board. Ask the students to count the squares. Show them the addition sentence 6 + 3 and say, "We have 6 squares. We need to add 3 more." Ask a student to place three more squares on the board. Tell the students to count on. Finally, ask them to count all the squares to confirm the total number of squares. Repeat this with other examples. Ask the students to look at this page. This time, do not use any concrete material. Tell the students to count the squares in the first addition sentence. Then, direct them to the second addition sentence. Tell them to trace and color the additional squares. For the third addition sentence, get them to tell you how many squares should be drawn.

Draw the correct number of ☐.
Write the numbers.

$1 + 5 =$ 6

2 + 2 = ☐

3 + 3 = ☐

4 + 1 = ☐

2 + 5 = ☐

4 + 6 = ☐

7 + 4 = ☐

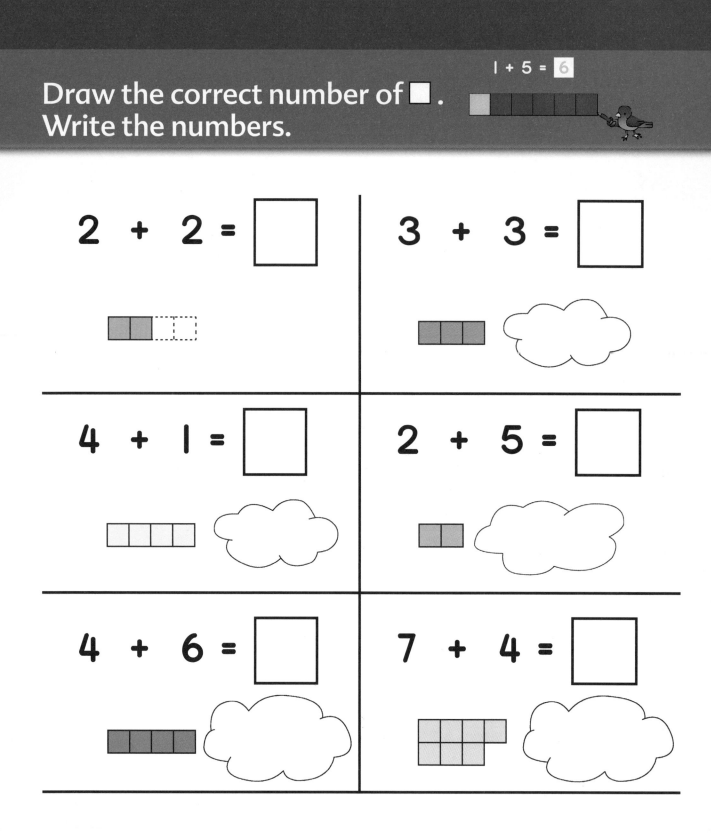

Development:
Tell the students to look at the first addition sentence on this page. Lead them to say, "There are 2 squares. Add 2 more." Then, ask them to add the squares by drawing two more. Tell the students to count on to get the answer. Then, ask them to count all the squares to confirm the answer.

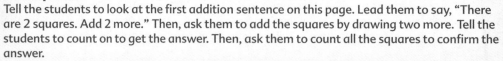

Activities 4 and 5, pages 48-53

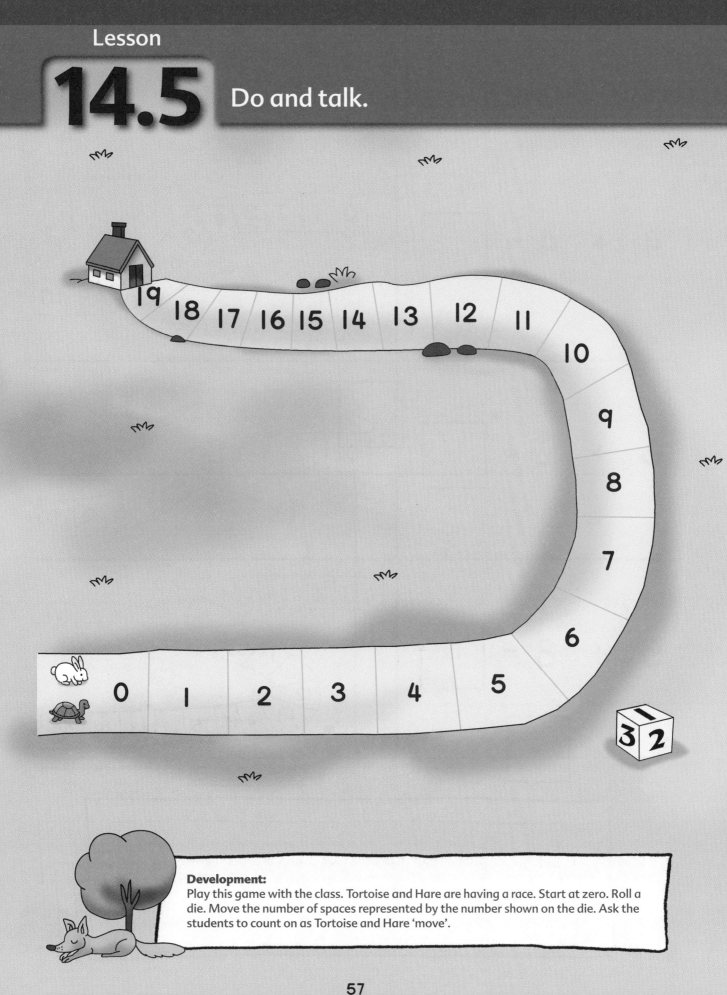

Development:
Play this game with the class. Tortoise and Hare are having a race. Start at zero. Roll a die. Move the number of spaces represented by the number shown on the die. Ask the students to count on as Tortoise and Hare 'move'.

Add.
Write the numbers.

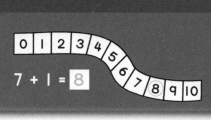

$7 + 1 = \boxed{8}$

$4 + 4 = \boxed{}$

$6 + 2 = \boxed{}$

$5 + 8 = \boxed{}$

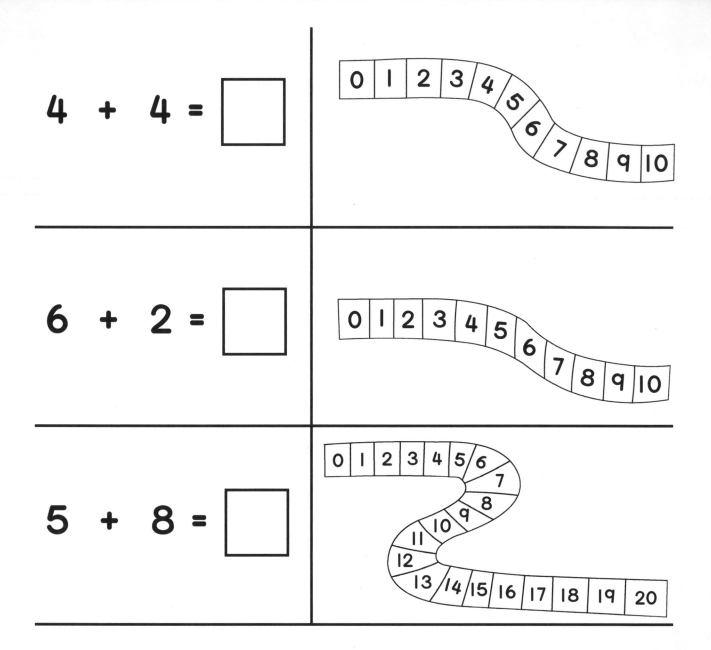

Development:
Draw the number chart on the board. Write an addition sentence on the board,
e.g. 3 + 7 = ☐. Point to the number chart as you say, "We are at 3. Let's move 7 more steps.
Where are we now?" Tell the students to look at this page. Give each student some counters.
Ask them to use the number chart to find the answers. Tell them to place a counter on the
number chart to indicate the first number of the addition sentence, e.g. 4. Then, ask them to
count on to add and to place another counter on the number chart to indicate the answer,
e.g. 8.

Development:
Put up six identical objects on the board. Ask six students to remove the objects one at a time. Ensure that there is nothing else on the board. Ask the class, "How many things are there on the board now? Which number can we use to describe what is on the board now?" Ask the students to tell a story that describes the picture on this page. Ask them why the fox looks full . Tell the students to describe the contents of the plate. Ask them for the number that describes what is on the plate after the fox has eaten. Show the class the numeral 0.

Add.
Write the numbers.

$2 + 0 = \boxed{2}$

$6 + 0 = \boxed{}$

$4 + 0 = \boxed{}$

$0 + 8 = \boxed{}$

Development:
Ask the students to describe the contents of the plates, boxes and trays. For each question, tell the students to count the food items to find how many there are altogether. Then, guide the students to complete the addition sentence. Ask them, "What do you notice about the answers?" Ask the students to tell you the answers to these sums: $7 + 0$, $9 + 0$, $0 + 2$, $8 + 0$

Development:
Organize a game. Place a stack of cards face down on the table. There are two players. Each player opens one card. They have to guess if the total shown on both cards is more or less than ten. Encourage them to do so without counting. The player who gives the correct answer first takes both cards. The winner is the player with more cards after a few rounds. Later, play the game again. However, this time the players have to add and tell the exact total of the numbers on both cards. The player who gives the correct answer first takes both cards. Count the number of cards to decide the winner.

Add.
Write the numbers.

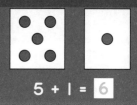

5 + 1 = 6

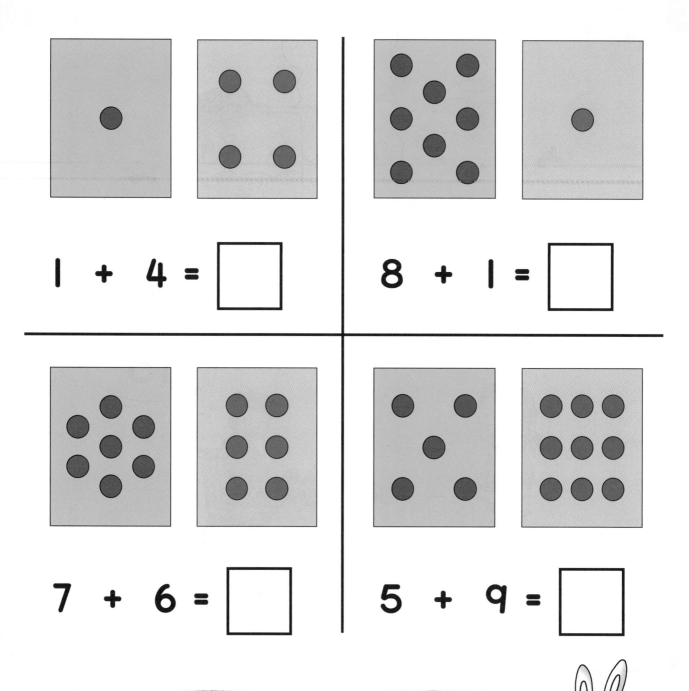

1 + 4 = ☐

8 + 1 = ☐

7 + 6 = ☐

5 + 9 = ☐

Development:
Place any two cards on the board. Ask two students to write the number that each card shows. Write '+' and '=' to form an addition sentence. Say, "There is 1 red dot and 1 green dot. How many dots are there altogether?" Tell the students to look at this page. Ask them to tell you how many dots there are altogether as they complete the addition sentence.

Add.
Write the numbers.

3 + 1 = 4

5 + 2 = ☐

3 + 6 = ☐

Add.
Write the numbers.

4 + 3 = 7

8 + 7 = ☐

4 + 6 = ☐

| 0 | 1 | 2 | 3 | 4 | 5 | 6 | 7 | 8 | 9 | 10 | 11 | 12 | 13 | 14 | 15 | 16 | 17 | 18 | 19 | 20 |

Draw the correct number of ▪ or ●.
Write the numbers.

3 + 5 = 8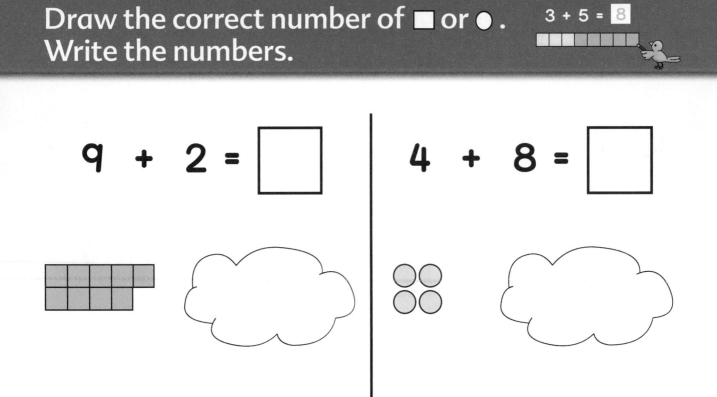

9 + 2 = ☐   4 + 8 = ☐

Add.
Write the numbers.

4 + 5 = 9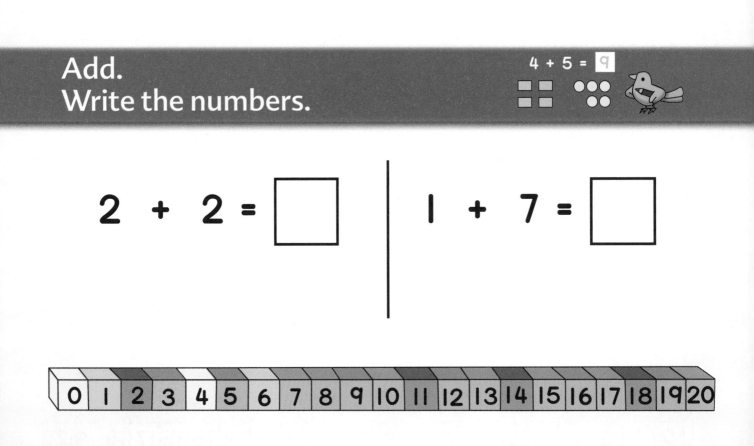

2 + 2 = ☐   1 + 7 = ☐

| 0 | 1 | 2 | 3 | 4 | 5 | 6 | 7 | 8 | 9 | 10 | 11 | 12 | 13 | 14 | 15 | 16 | 17 | 18 | 19 | 20 |

15.1   Look and talk.

Introduction:
Bring five balloons to class. Tell the students to look at this page. Have them talk about what they see in the picture and predict what could happen next.

Look and talk.

Development:
Ask two students to burst one balloon each. Say, "There were 5 balloons. 2 burst. Now there are 3 balloons." Tell the students to look at this page. Then, have them talk about what has happened to the balloons, birds and mice as compared to the previous page. Say, e.g. "There were 4 mice. 1 ran away. How many mice are still here?"

Cross out (✗) the burst balloon.
Write the numbers.

2 burst. 2 🎈 left

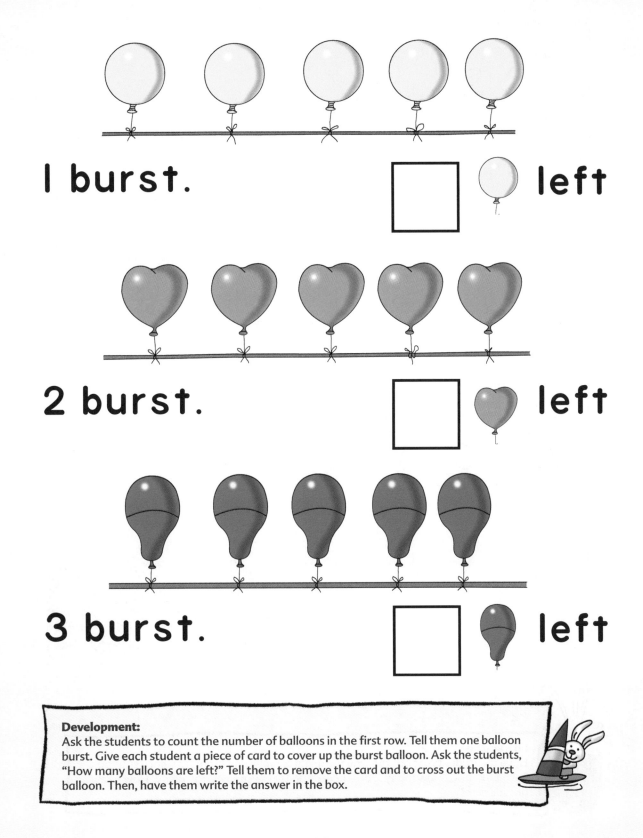

1 burst. ⬜ 🎈 left

2 burst. ⬜ 💜 left

3 burst. ⬜ 🎈 left

Development:
Ask the students to count the number of balloons in the first row. Tell them one balloon burst. Give each student a piece of card to cover up the burst balloon. Ask the students, "How many balloons are left?" Tell them to remove the card and to cross out the burst balloon. Then, have them write the answer in the box.

Activity I, pages 54-55

Introduction:
Have the students act out the way the animals move and dramatize each situation. Each time, ask, "How many ... are there at first? How many ... ran away? How many ... are still here?"

Look and talk.

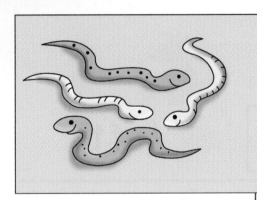

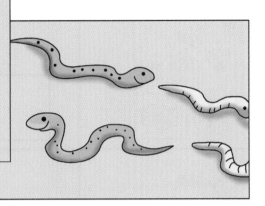

Development:
Have the students act out the way the animals move and dramatize each situation. Have them tell you what they think happened in each picture. Then, ask, "How many ... are still here?"

Cross out (X) what the animal eats.
Write the numbers.

🐭 eats 2 🐝. 2 🐝 left

🐭 eats 1 🧀 .   ☐ 🧀 left

🐱 eats 4 🐟 .   ☐ 🐟 left

🐰 eats 3 🥕 .   ☐ 🥕 left

🐿 eats 3 🌰 .   ☐ 🌰 left

Introduction:
Have a volunteer act as an animal, e.g. a frog. Show the class a number of food items, e.g. a picture of four flies. Say, "The frog eats ... flies." Remove the correct number of flies from the board. Tell the students to count the number of flies left. Repeat this with other animals and food items.

Development:
Tell the students a story about the mouse eating a piece of cheese. Tell the students to cross out one piece of cheese. Ask them to count the number of pieces left. Repeat this with the other animals on this page.

15.3 Look and talk.

Introduction:
Have the students talk about things they do at the beach.
Development:
Ask the class, "How many buckets are there? 1 bucket is red. The rest are blue.
How many buckets are blue?" Repeat this with the children and shovels.

Color.
Write the numbers.

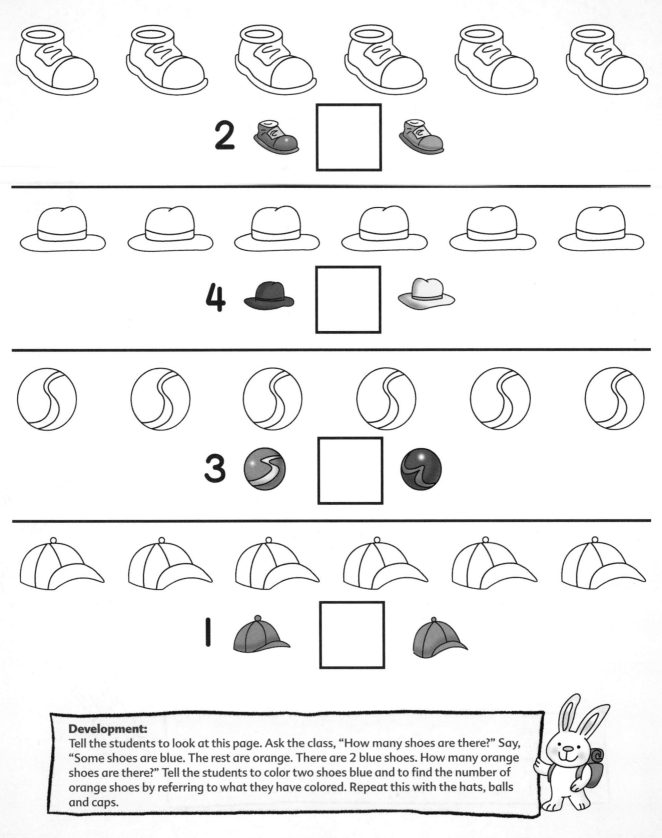

2

4

3

I

Development:
Tell the students to look at this page. Ask the class, "How many shoes are there?" Say, "Some shoes are blue. The rest are orange. There are 2 blue shoes. How many orange shoes are there?" Tell the students to color two shoes blue and to find the number of orange shoes by referring to what they have colored. Repeat this with the hats, balls and caps.

4 □

5 □   2 □

Introduction:
Have the students talk about the animals. Put up pictures of these animals on the board.
Say, e.g. "There are 4 lions. How many lionesses are there?"
Development:
Ask the students to count the number of each type of animal. Say, "There are 7 ... There
are ... How many ... are there?" Have the students count to find the answers.

Color.
Write the numbers.

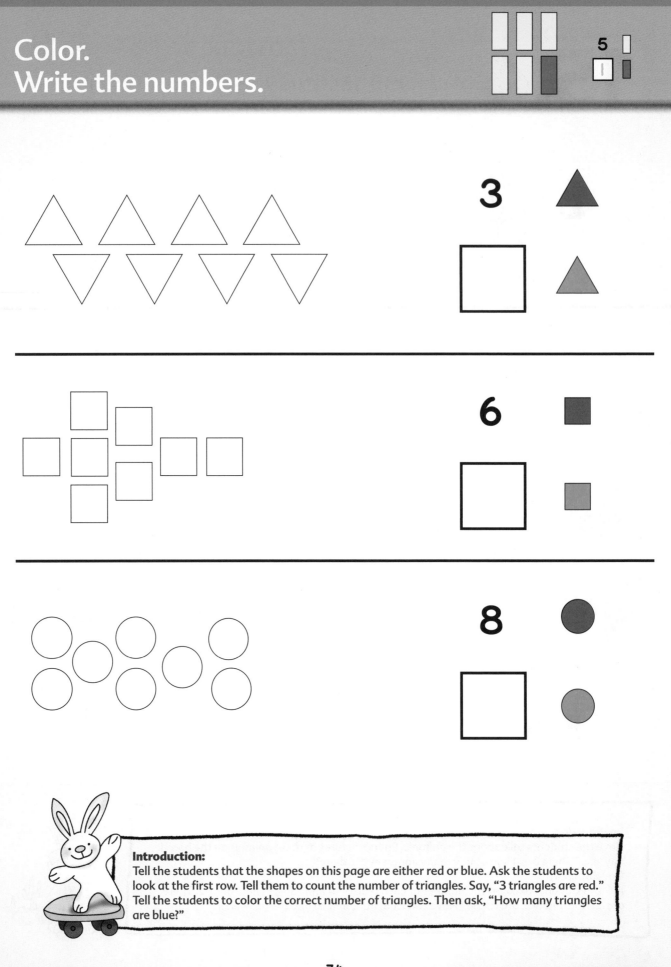

3

6

8

Introduction:
Tell the students that the shapes on this page are either red or blue. Ask the students to look at the first row. Tell them to count the number of triangles. Say, "3 triangles are red." Tell the students to color the correct number of triangles. Then ask, "How many triangles are blue?"

Activity 2, pages 56-57

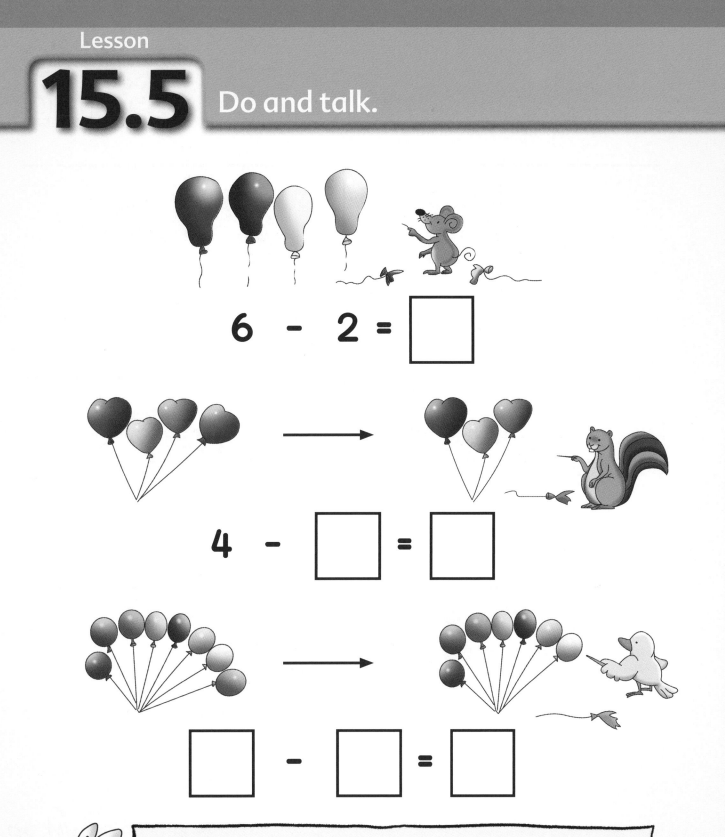

$$6 - 2 = \boxed{}$$

$$4 - \boxed{} = \boxed{}$$

$$\boxed{} - \boxed{} = \boxed{}$$

Introduction:
Show the class three balloons. Write '3' on the board. Ask a student to burst two balloons. Then, write the **subtraction sign** and '2' to show '3 – 2'. Ask, "How many balloons are left?" Finally, complete the **subtraction sentence** to show 3 – 2 = 1.
Development:
Tell the students to look at this page. Ask them to talk about each situation. Guide them to write the subtraction sentences.

Subtract.
Write the numbers.

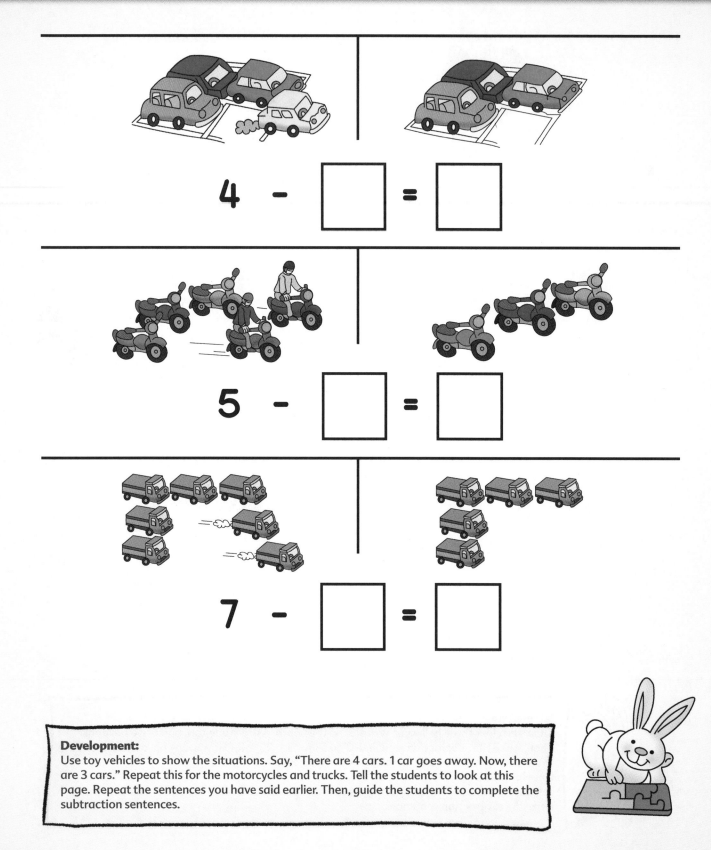

4 - [ ] = [ ]

5 - [ ] = [ ]

7 - [ ] = [ ]

Development:
Use toy vehicles to show the situations. Say, "There are 4 cars. 1 car goes away. Now, there are 3 cars." Repeat this for the motorcycles and trucks. Tell the students to look at this page. Repeat the sentences you have said earlier. Then, guide the students to complete the subtraction sentences.

Activity 3, pages 58-59

15.6 Look and talk.

Introduction:
Have the students look at this page. Ask the students to talk about the food items on this page. Allow them to talk about the food items they like and what they do not like.

Development:
Have the students talk about what the boy is doing. Ask the students "How many apples are there at first? How many apples does the boy eat? How many apples are there now?" Write the subtraction sentence at the same time. Then, encourage the students to describe the situation again by referring to the subtraction sentence. Have different students select a food item from this page and make up a situation. Guide the students to write a subtraction sentence for each situation.

Cross out (X) the correct number of buttons. Write the numbers.

5 - 5 = 0

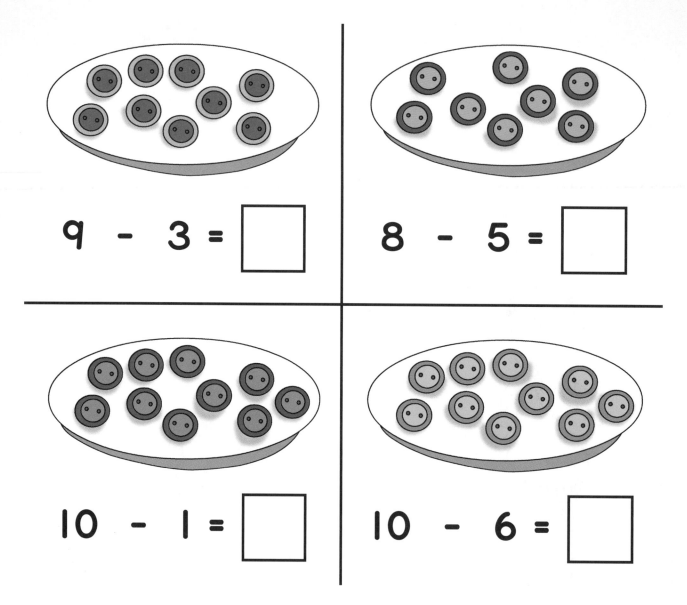

9 - 3 = ☐

8 - 5 = ☐

10 - 1 = ☐

10 - 6 = ☐

Consolidation:
Have the students look at this page. Ask them to talk about the situations shown. Emphasize the connection between each situation and the subtraction sentence. Tell them to complete the subtraction sentence. Repeat this for the next three questions.

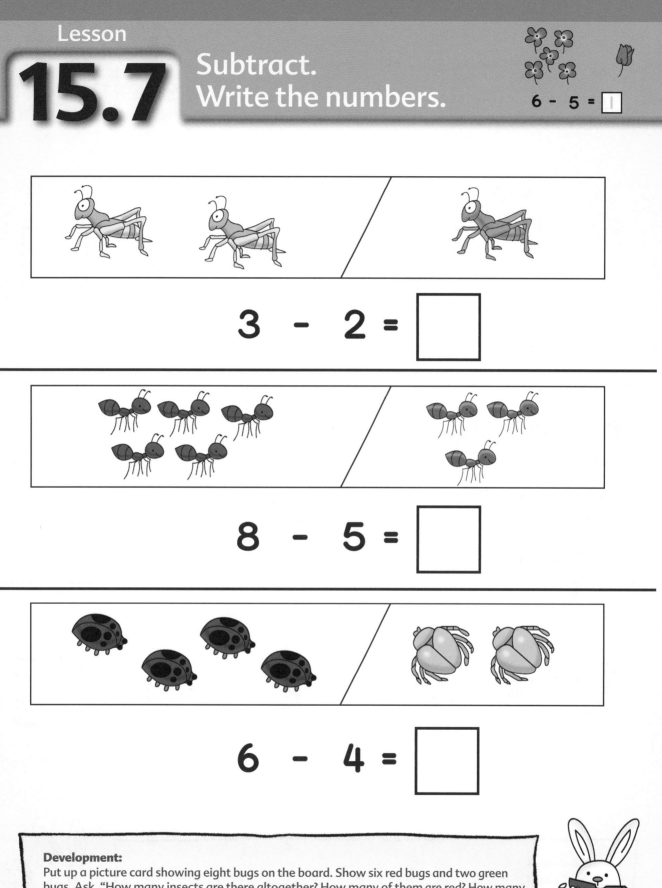

3 - 2 = ☐

8 - 5 = ☐

6 - 4 = ☐

Development:
Put up a picture card showing eight bugs on the board. Show six red bugs and two green
bugs. Ask, "How many insects are there altogether? How many of them are red? How many
of them are green?" Use the situation to write a subtraction sentence. Have the students
retell the situation using the subtraction sentence. Tell the students to look at this page.
Repeat this for the three situations on this page.

Color.
Write the numbers.

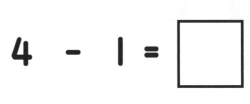

$$4 - 1 = \boxed{}$$

$$5 - 3 = \boxed{}$$

$$9 - 6 = \boxed{}$$

Consolidation:
Have the students look at this page. Lead the students to say, "There are 4 dolls altogether. 1 doll wears a red dress." Tell them to color one dress red. Then, ask, "How many dolls are wearing purple dresses?" Tell the students to complete the subtraction sentence. Have them use the subtraction sentence to describe the situation again. Repeat this for the next two questions.

Color.
Write the numbers.

8 - 1 = 7

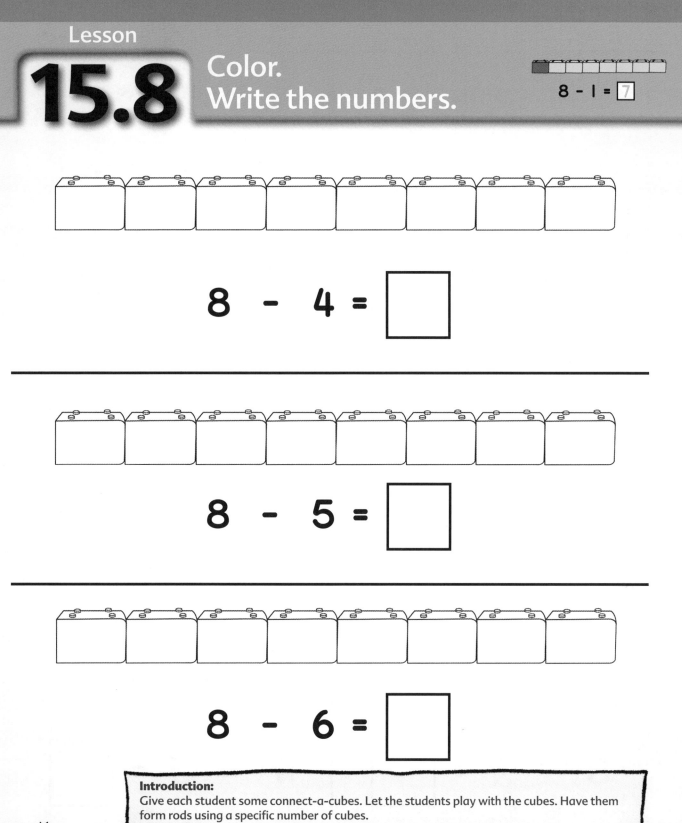

8 - 4 = ☐

8 - 5 = ☐

8 - 6 = ☐

Introduction:
Give each student some connect-a-cubes. Let the students play with the cubes. Have them form rods using a specific number of cubes.

Development:
Give each student some cubes in two different colors. Tell the students to form a rod using two colors. Tell them that they must use eight cubes altogether. Ask, "How many cubes are there altogether? How many of them are red? How many of them are blue?" Write the subtraction sentence on the board. Guide them to use the subtraction sentence to describe the situation again. Tell the students to look at this page. Have them use their cubes to show each subtraction sentence. Tell them to color the toy bricks and to complete the subtraction sentence. Repeat this for the next two questions.

Color.
Write the numbers.

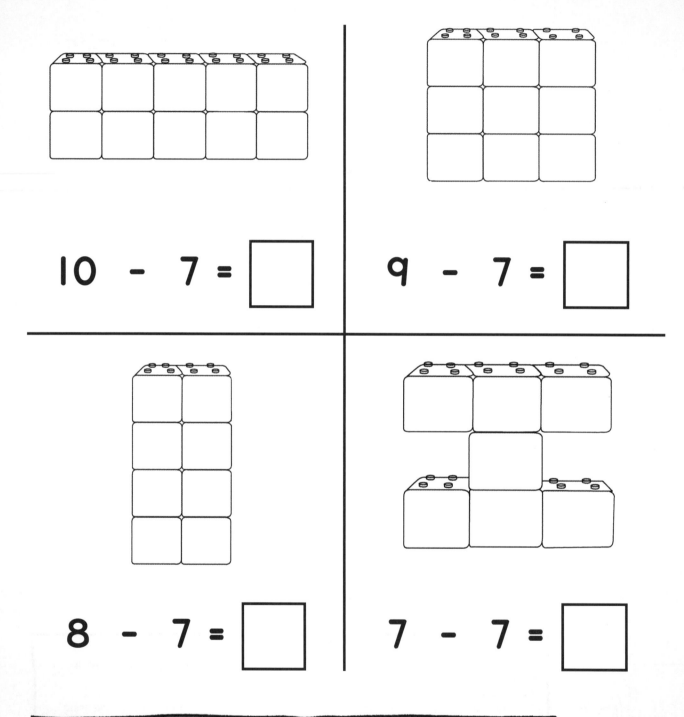

10 - 7 = ☐

9 - 7 = ☐

8 - 7 = ☐

7 - 7 = ☐

Consolidation:
Have the students look at this page. Say, "There are 10 toy bricks altogether. 7 of them are red. How many are purple?" Tell the students to color the toy bricks and to complete the subtraction sentence. Have them use the subtraction sentence to describe the situation again. Repeat this for the next three questions.

Activity 5, page 61

Review

Cross out (X) the correct number of buttons. Write the numbers.

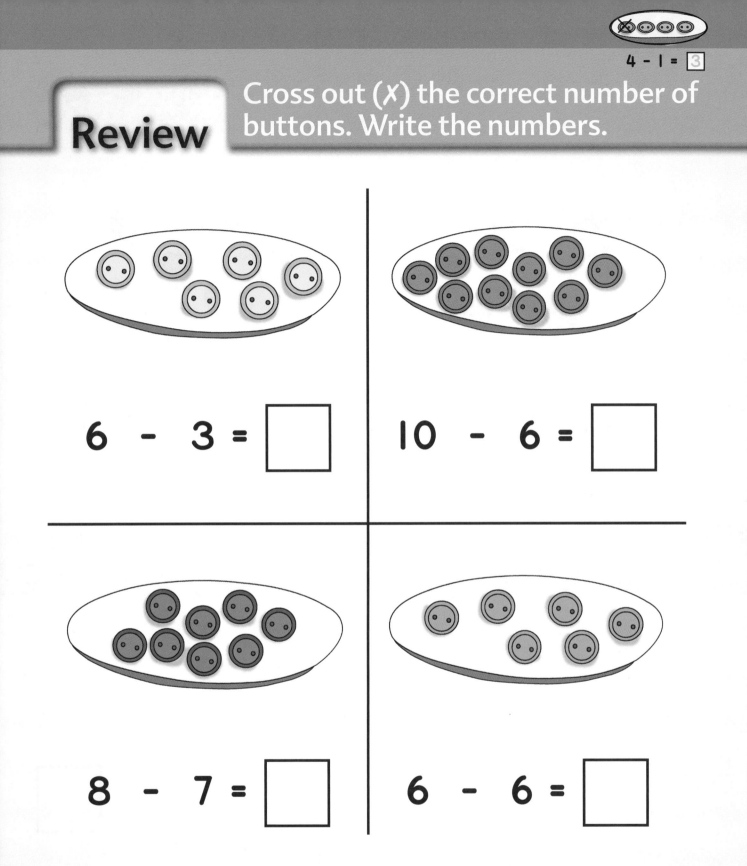

6 − 3 = ☐

10 − 6 = ☐

8 − 7 = ☐

6 − 6 = ☐

Cross out (X) the correct number of apples. Write the numbers.

2 - 1 = ☐

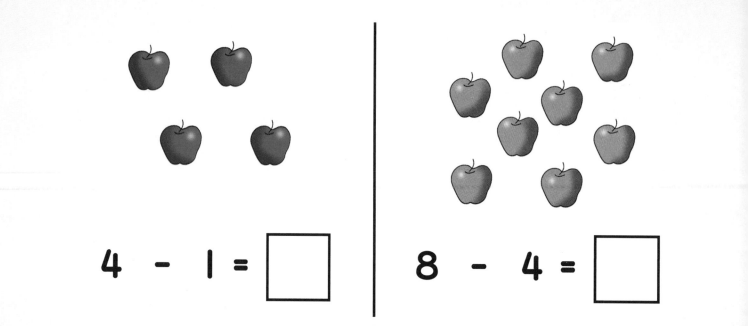

4 - 1 = ☐   8 - 4 = ☐

Color. Write the numbers.

3 - 2 = 1

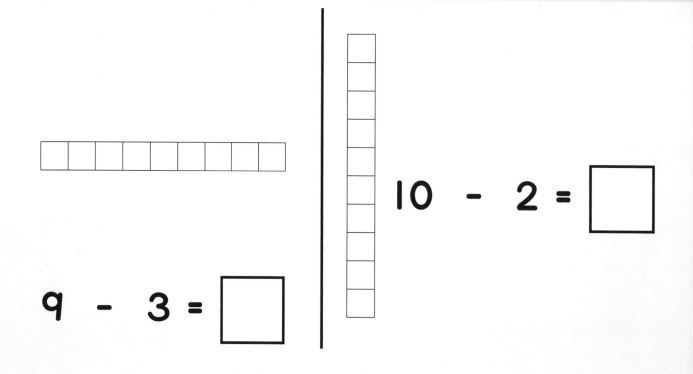

10 - 2 = ☐

9 - 3 = ☐

16.1 Do and talk.

5 + 2 = ☐   5 - 2 = ☐

Two Little Dicky Birds

Development:
Give each student five items. Ask them to tell you what happens when two are removed. Ask them to tell you what happens when two more are added. Have them act out a situation using these five items. Repeat this with a different number of items.

Have the students look at this page. Ask them to describe the first picture with five bees. Tell them two more bees fly to join the five. Ask them to tell you the total number of bees. Refer to 5 + 2 and say, "At first, there are 5 bees. 2 bees join them." Repeat this with 5 − 2.

Add and subtract.
Write the numbers.

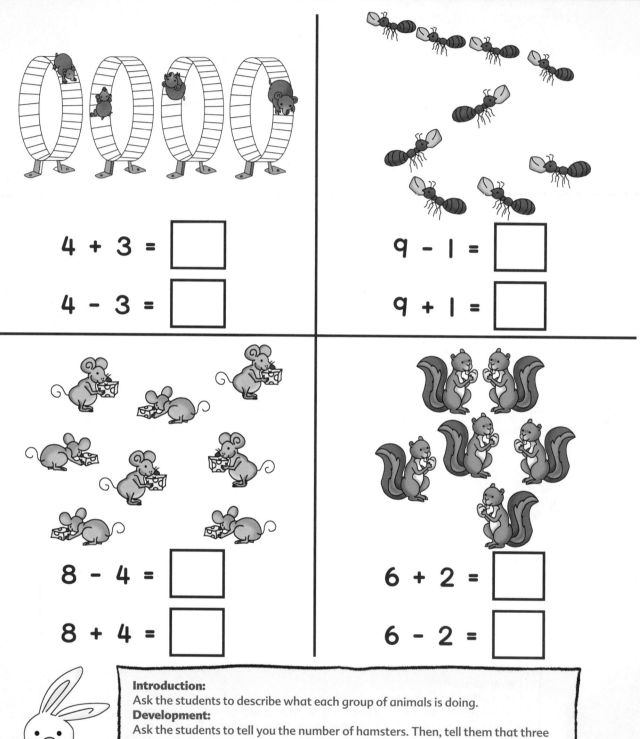

4 + 3 = ☐

4 - 3 = ☐

9 - 1 = ☐

9 + 1 = ☐

8 - 4 = ☐

8 + 4 = ☐

6 + 2 = ☐

6 - 2 = ☐

Introduction:
Ask the students to describe what each group of animals is doing.
Development:
Ask the students to tell you the number of hamsters. Then, tell them that three more hamsters join the group. Refer to 4 + 3 and repeat the story. Tell the students to **count on** using counters or their fingers. Refer to the original situation again. Now, tell them that three hamsters left the group. Refer to 4 — 3 and repeat the story. Get the students to cover the hamsters that left the group using their fingers. Alternatively, get the students to do the subtraction using counters.

Activity l. pages 62-63

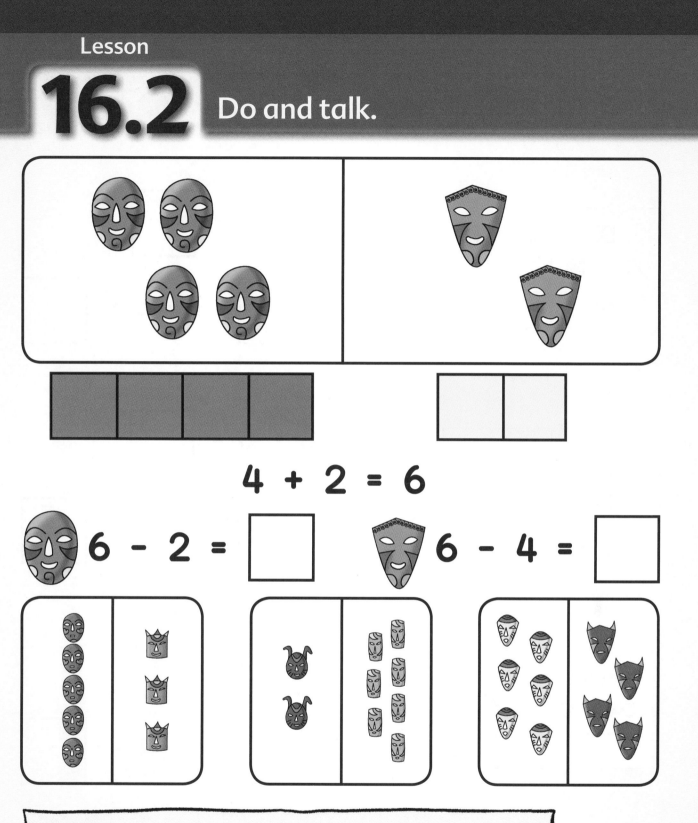

$$4 + 2 = 6$$

$$6 - 2 = \boxed{}$$

$$6 - 4 = \boxed{}$$

Introduction:
Bring different kinds of masks to class. Show these to the students. Ask them to describe these masks.

Development:
Place four masks on the board. Arrange the masks as shown in the first picture. Ask the students to tell you the number of masks needed to make a total of six. Tell them to verify their answers by putting up two more masks on the board. Use connect-a-cubes to model the situation. Then, ask them what happens when two are removed, and when four are removed. Repeat this for the other three situations.

Add and subtract.
Write the numbers.

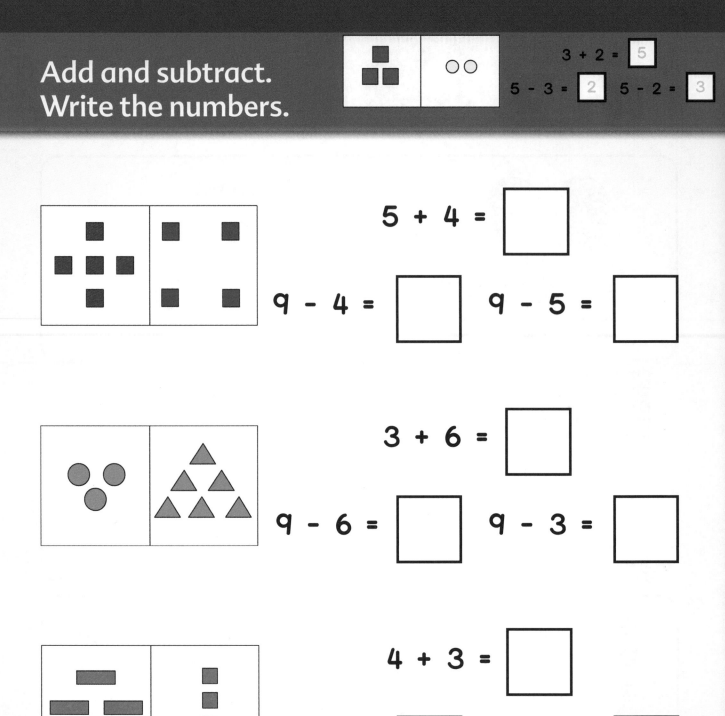

5 + 4 = ☐

9 - 4 = ☐   9 - 5 = ☐

3 + 6 = ☐

9 - 6 = ☐   9 - 3 = ☐

4 + 3 = ☐

7 - 3 = ☐   7 - 4 = ☐

Development:
Show the class a picture card depicting the first picture on this page. Get the students to count on to find the answer to 5 + 4. Cover the right side of the card. Ask the students to find the answer to 9 − 4. Repeat this for 9 − 5.

Introduction:
Tell the students to describe what they see on this page. Ask them to describe what the animals are doing. Have them describe the colors of the flowers and sizes of the ducks.

Development:
Have the students solve a few simple problems presented orally. Ask, "How many flowers are there? How many animals are there? How many types of animals are there?" Encourage the students to make up number stories using the picture shown on this page. Guide them to use the structure, "There are ... There are ... How many ....?" to model the **part-whole** situations.

Listen. Add or subtract.
Then complete the number sentences.

Ben and Meg have ☐ 🥨.

There are ☐ 🍎.

She hides ☐ ❀.

Development:
Present each problem situation orally. For the first picture, say, "Ben has 2 pretzels. Meg has 5 pretzels. How many pretzels do they have altogether?" For the second picture, say, "There are 8 apples in this box. 4 are red. The rest are green. How many green apples are there?" For the third picture, say, "Tarsha has 9 flowers. How many flowers is she hiding behind her back?" Give each student counters to represent the situations. Some students may draw to solve the problems. Others may count all or count on. Encourage students to share the strategy they have used. Finally, guide them to solve the problems by completing the number sentences.

16.4 Look and talk.

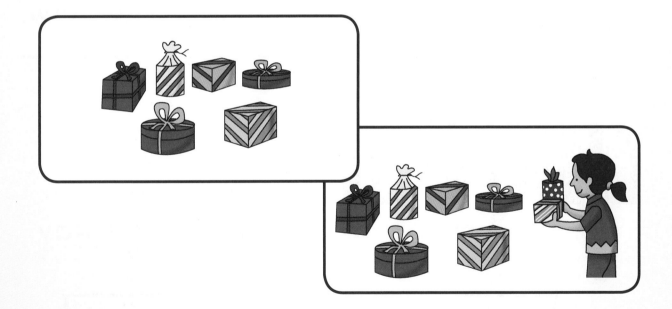

Introduction:
Have the students talk about birthday parties they have had or have attended.
Development:
Guide the students to make up problem situations using this page. Encourage them to say, "At first, there are ... Then, ... How many ...?" to model different situations.

Listen. Add or subtract.
Then write the numbers.

☐ 🛡️ are still here.

There are ☐ 🐻 now.

☐ 💂 march away.

Introduction:
Get the students to talk about their favorite toys.

Development:
Present each problem situation orally. For the first picture, say, "There are 5 knights. 2 knights march away. How many knights are still here?" For the second picture, say, "There are 4 teddy bears. 2 join the group. How many teddy bears are there?" For the third picture, say, "At first, there are 7 tin soldiers. Some march away. Now, only 2 are still here. How many tin soldiers march away?" Give each student counters to represent the situations.

Review

Add or subtract.
Write the numbers.

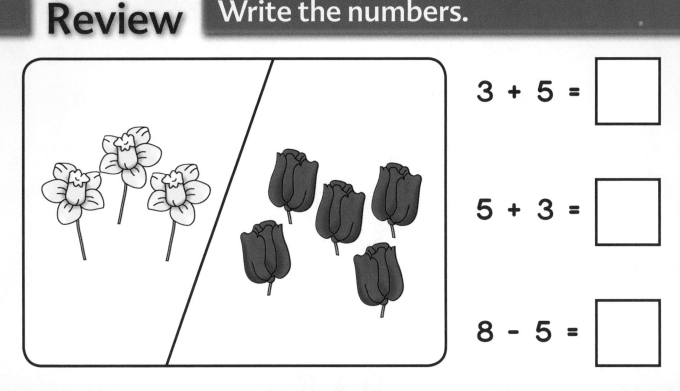

3 + 5 = ☐

5 + 3 = ☐

8 - 5 = ☐

Listen. Add or subtract.
Then write the numbers.

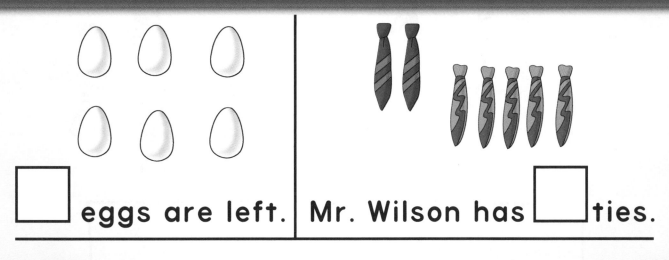

☐ eggs are left. | Mr. Wilson has ☐ ties.

Development:
Present the problem situations at the bottom of this page orally. For the second question, say, "Mother cooks 6 eggs. Jon eats 2 eggs. How many eggs are left?" For the third question, say, "Mr. Wilson has 2 red ties and 5 blue ties. How many ties does he have altogether?"

17.1 Look and talk.

Introduction:
Show the students a basketful of toy soldiers. Get them to guess the number of toy soldiers without counting.

Development:
Have the students count to check their guesses. Repeat this with different numbers of toy soldiers. Arrange the toy soldiers in groups of ten as shown on this page. Ask the students to tell you the number of toy soldiers again. Ask them to say if it is easier to tell the number of toy soldiers now than before. Encourage them to say why. Tell the students to look at this page. Ask them to count the number of soldiers in each group. Ask them to tell you the number of soldiers in each group. Finally, get them to tell you the number of soldiers on this page.

Count.
Write the numbers.

Tens	Ones
1	2

12	🍎

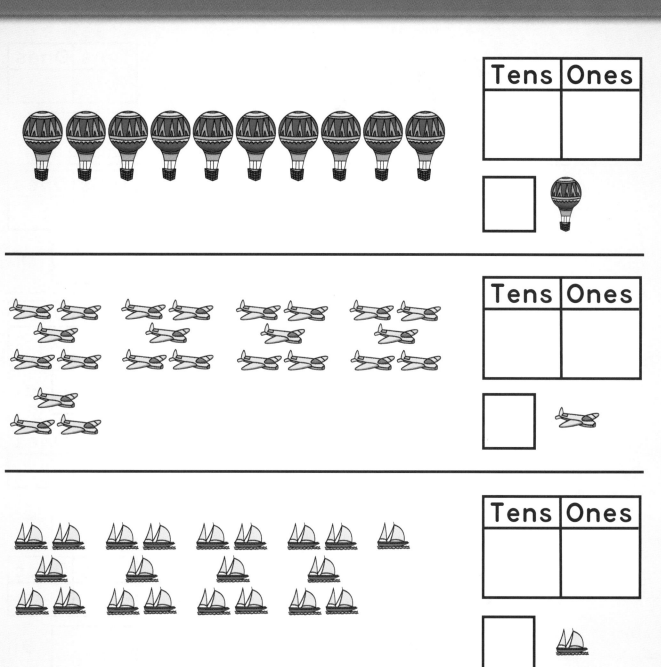

Tens	Ones

	🎈

Tens	Ones

	✈

Tens	Ones

	⛵

Development:
Show cutouts of ten hot-air balloons on the board. Arrange the hot-air balloons in a group of ten. Get the students to tell you the number of hot-air balloons. Say, "There is 1 group of ten hot-air balloons." Repeat with 23 airplanes and 2 ships. Say, "There are 2 groups of ten airplanes and 3 more." and "There are 2 groups of ten ships." Get the students to look at this page. Show them how to write 1 group of ten in the **place value chart**. Also, show them how the digits in the place value chart form the numerals 10, 23 and 21.

Activity 1, pages 71-72

17.2

Count.
Write the numbers.

Tens	Ones
1	4

14 🍎

Tens	Ones

[ ] 🔵

Tens	Ones

[ ] 🔵

Tens	Ones

[ ] 🔵

Tens	Ones

[ ] 🔵

Tens	Ones

[ ] 🔵

Introduction:
Organize a relay race. Each team has four students. Give each team 23 beads and some string. When you say, "Go!", two students from each team have to form a string of ten beads. When they are done, the next two will do the same. The first team to finish the activity correctly wins.

Consolidation:
Refer to the strings of beads the students have made. Guide the students to say, "There are 2 groups of ten beads and 5 more. There are 25 beads." Tell them to look at this page. Guide them to say, "There are ... groups of ten beads and ... more." as they fill in the place value chart. Then, get them to say the number aloud as they write the numerals.

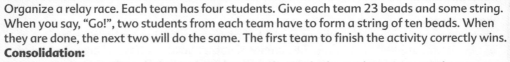

Count.
Write the numbers.

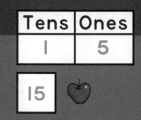

Tens	Ones
1	5

15	🍎

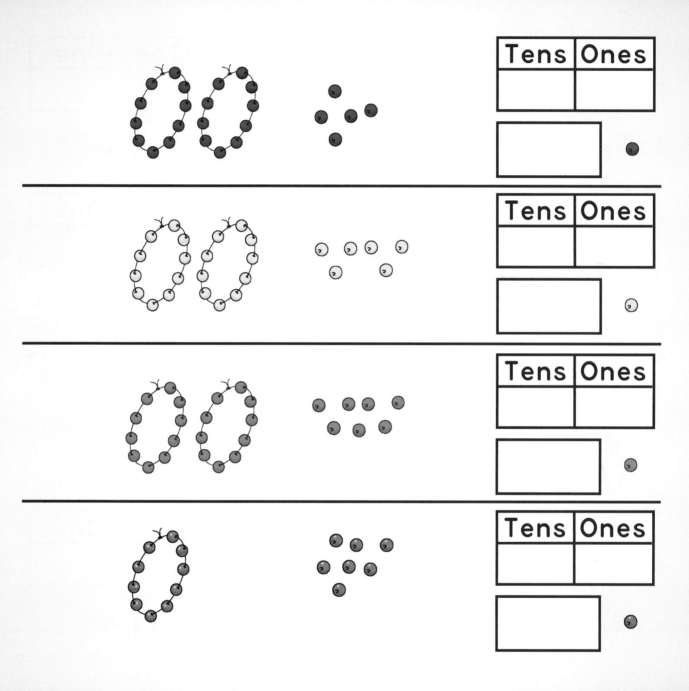

Tens	Ones

	•

Tens	Ones

	•

Tens	Ones

	•

Tens	Ones

	•

Consolidation:
Tell the students to look at this page. Guide them to say, "There are ... groups of ten beads and ... more." as they fill in the place value chart. Then, ask them to say the number aloud as they write the numerals.

Count.
Write the numbers.

Tens	Ones
1	6

16 🍎

Tens	Ones

Tens	Ones

Tens	Ones

Tens	Ones

Consolidation:
Guide the students to say, "There are 2 branches of ten leaves and ... more. There are ....
leaves." Tell them to look at this page. Ask them to say, "There are ... branches of ten leaves
and ... more." as they fill in the place value chart. Then, ask them to say the number aloud as
they write the numerals.

Count.
Write the numbers.

Tens	Ones
1	7

17

Tens	Ones

Tens	Ones

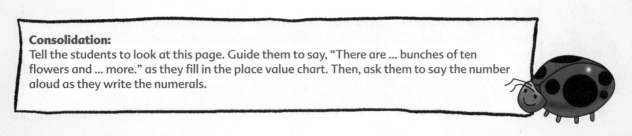

Consolidation:
Tell the students to look at this page. Guide them to say, "There are ... bunches of ten flowers and ... more." as they fill in the place value chart. Then, ask them to say the number aloud as they write the numerals.

Introduction:
Tell the students to work in groups. Ask them to fill three ten frames with buttons.
Development:
Give each student between 20 and 30 buttons and three ten frames. Tell them to fill these frames and tell you the number of buttons they have. Guide them to say, "I have ... groups of ten and ... more. I have ... buttons." Next, give each group between 20 and 30 buttons spread out on a large piece of paper. Get them to use crayons to circle ten buttons. Ask them to tell you the number of buttons they have. Tell the students to look at this page. Tell them to circle ten eggs/sticks and say, "There are ... groups of ten eggs/sticks and ... more. There are ... eggs/sticks."

Count.
Write the numbers.

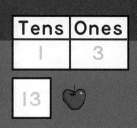

Tens	Ones
1	3

13 🍎

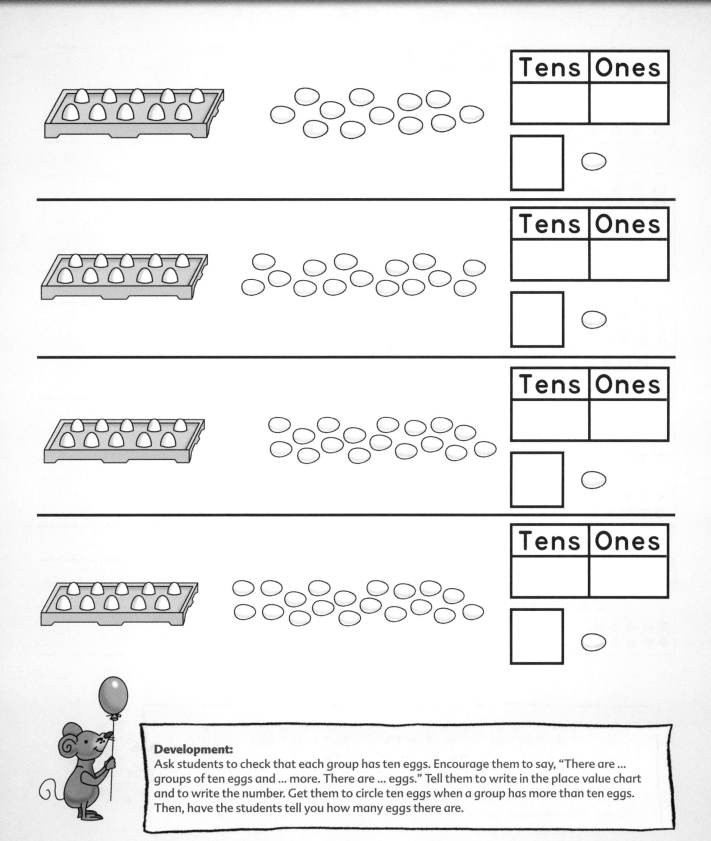

Tens	Ones

Tens	Ones

Tens	Ones

Tens	Ones

Development:
Ask students to check that each group has ten eggs. Encourage them to say, "There are ...
groups of ten eggs and ... more. There are ... eggs." Tell them to write in the place value chart
and to write the number. Get them to circle ten eggs when a group has more than ten eggs.
Then, have the students tell you how many eggs there are.

17.5

Write the numbers.

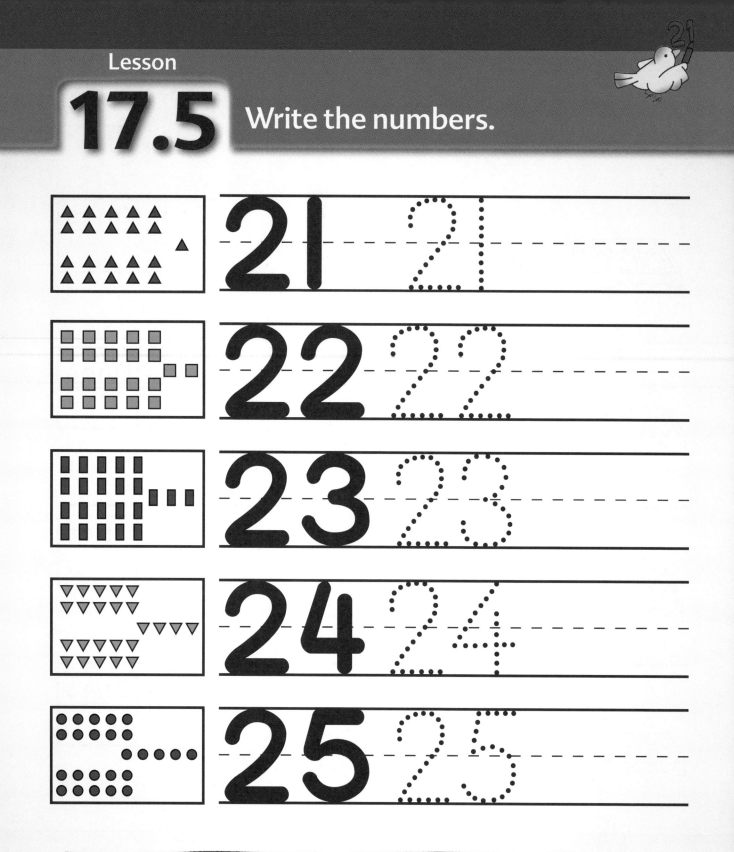

21 21

22 22

23 23

24 24

25 25

Development:
Put up cards each showing between 20 and 30 items. Tell the students to look at this page. Point at a number. Ask the students to look for the card that shows the correct number of items. Show them how to write the numerals. Show the numerals on the board. Have a few students trace the numerals on the board using their fingers. Finally, tell them to write the numbers on this page using the dotted lines for guidance. Repeat for the other numbers.

Write the numbers.

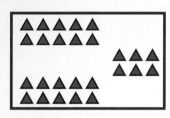 **26**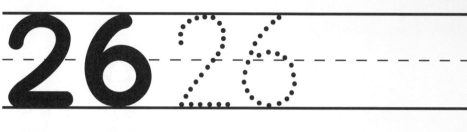

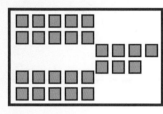 **27**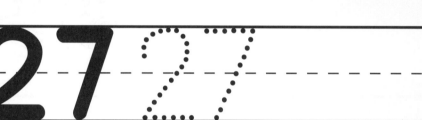

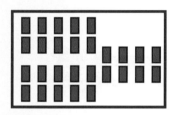 **28**

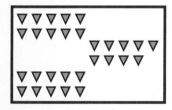 **29**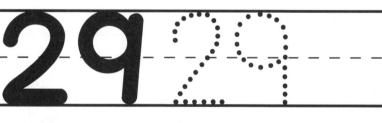

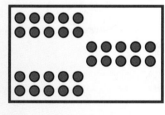 **30**

Development:
Put up cards each showing between 20 and 30 items. Tell the students to look at this page. Point at a number. Ask the students to look for the card that shows the correct number of items. Show them how to write the numerals. Show the numerals on the board. Have a few students trace the numerals on the board using their fingers. Finally, tell them to write the numbers on this page using the dotted lines for guidance. Repeat for the other numbers.

Activity 2, pages 73-74

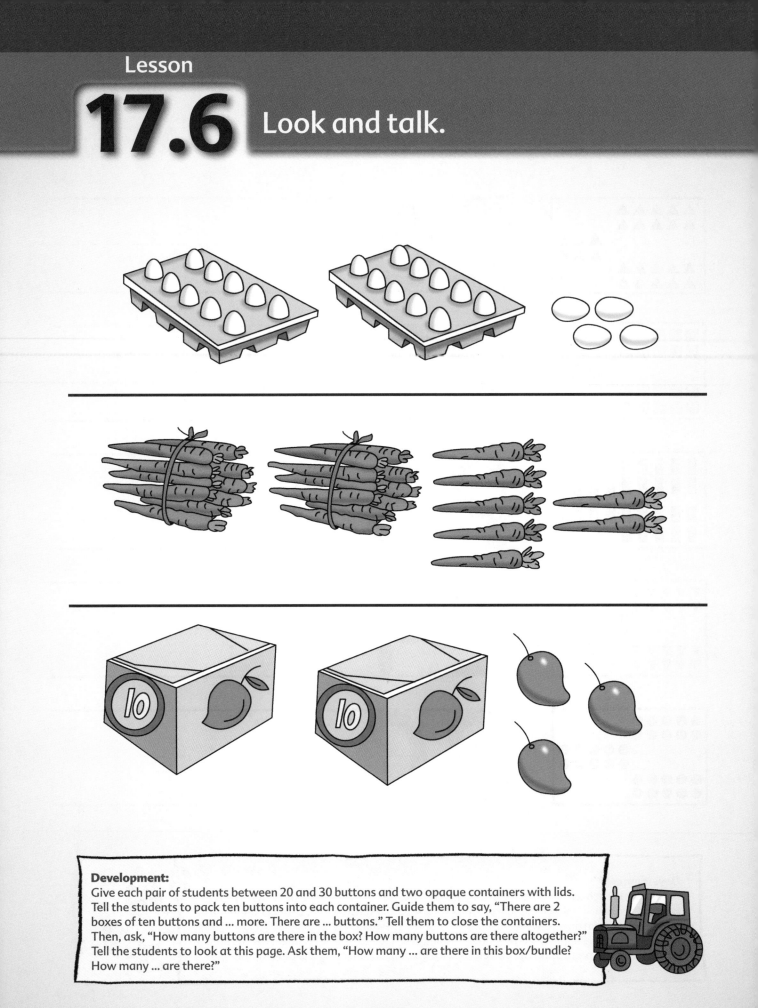

Development:
Give each pair of students between 20 and 30 buttons and two opaque containers with lids. Tell the students to pack ten buttons into each container. Guide them to say, "There are 2 boxes of ten buttons and ... more. There are ... buttons." Tell them to close the containers. Then, ask, "How many buttons are there in the box? How many buttons are there altogether?" Tell the students to look at this page. Ask them, "How many ... are there in this box/bundle? How many ... are there?"

Circle groups of 10.
Write the numbers.

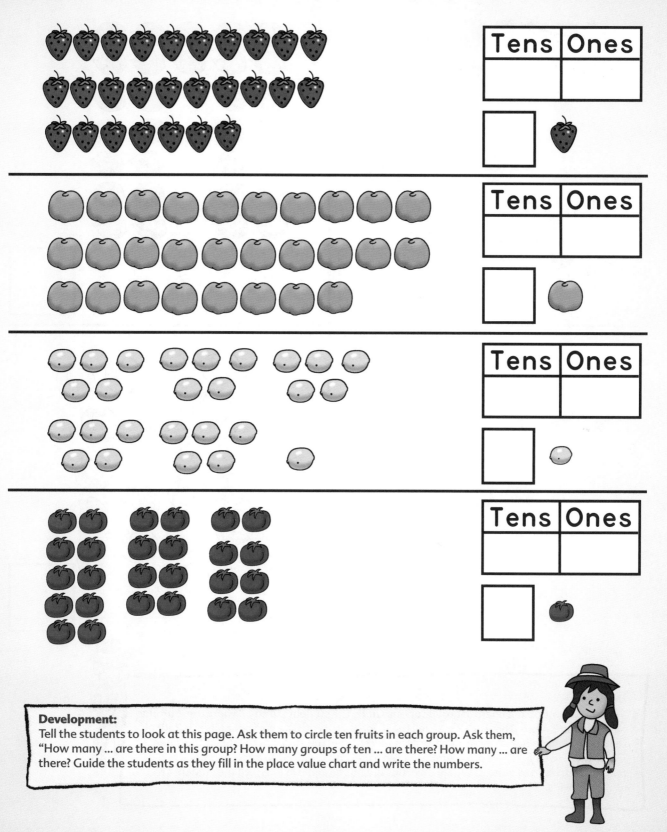

Tens	Ones
2	3

23

Tens	Ones

Tens	Ones

Tens	Ones

Tens	Ones

Development:
Tell the students to look at this page. Ask them to circle ten fruits in each group. Ask them, "How many ... are there in this group? How many groups of ten ... are there? How many ... are there? Guide the students as they fill in the place value chart and write the numbers.

17.7

Count.
Write the numbers.

24

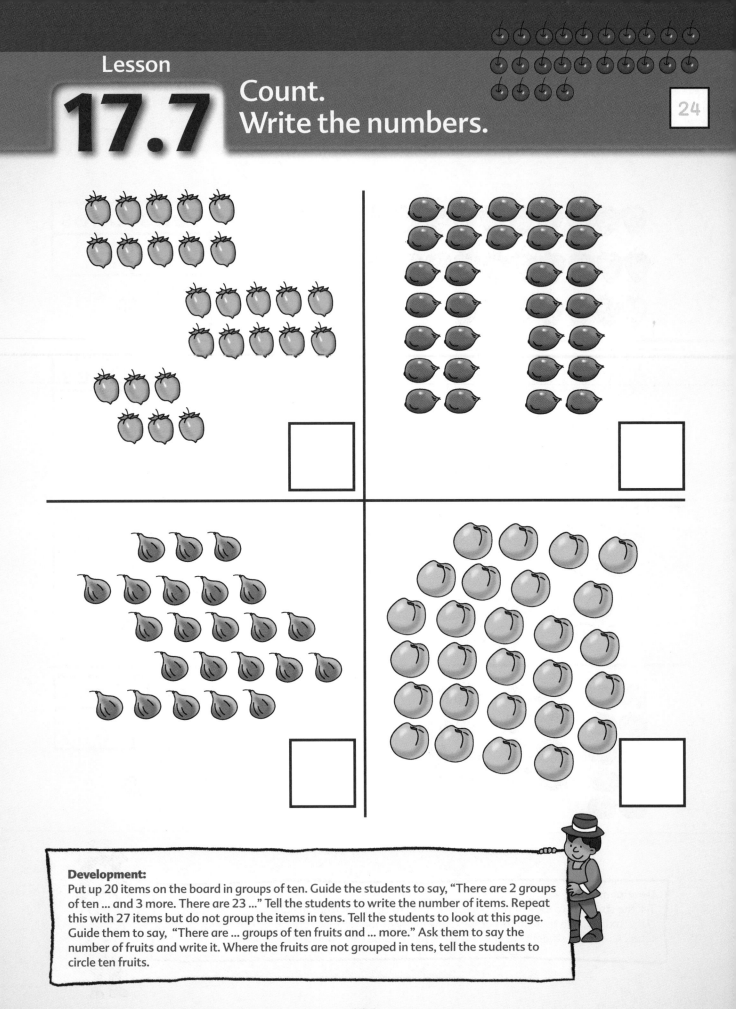

Development:
Put up 20 items on the board in groups of ten. Guide the students to say, "There are 2 groups of ten ... and 3 more. There are 23 ..." Tell the students to write the number of items. Repeat this with 27 items but do not group the items in tens. Tell the students to look at this page. Guide them to say, "There are ... groups of ten fruits and ... more." Ask them to say the number of fruits and write it. Where the fruits are not grouped in tens, tell the students to circle ten fruits.

Count.
Write the numbers.

Consolidation:
Encourage students to complete this page independently. Guide students who require help.

17.8 Color.

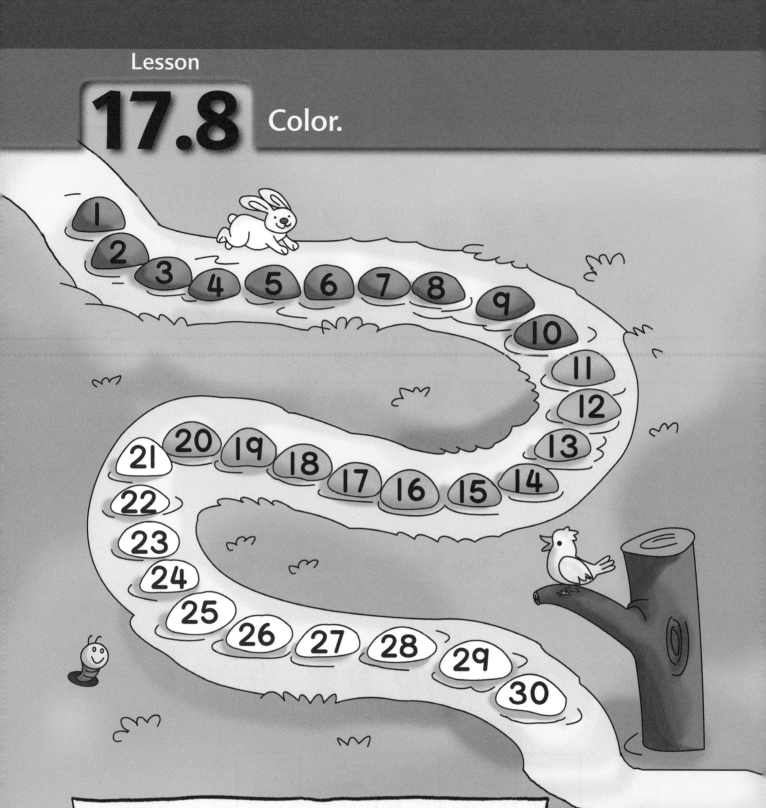

Introduction:
Play a game where students recite numbers to 20 in order but say, "Beep" each time the digit 4 appears in the number, e.g. 4 or 14. When the students have recited numbers to 20, have them play the game again with the numbers in reverse order.

Development:
Play the same game with numbers to 30. Then, have the students get into teams. Each team gets numeral cards with the numbers 1 to 30. Tell the teams to arrange the cards in the correct order in the shortest time possible. After the game, tell the students to look at this page. Say a number between 20 and 30. Tell the students to look for the number on this page and to color the correct stone. Finally, have them say the numbers 1 to 30 in order, and again in reverse order.

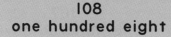

Fill in the missing numbers.

Activities 3 and 4, pages 75-77

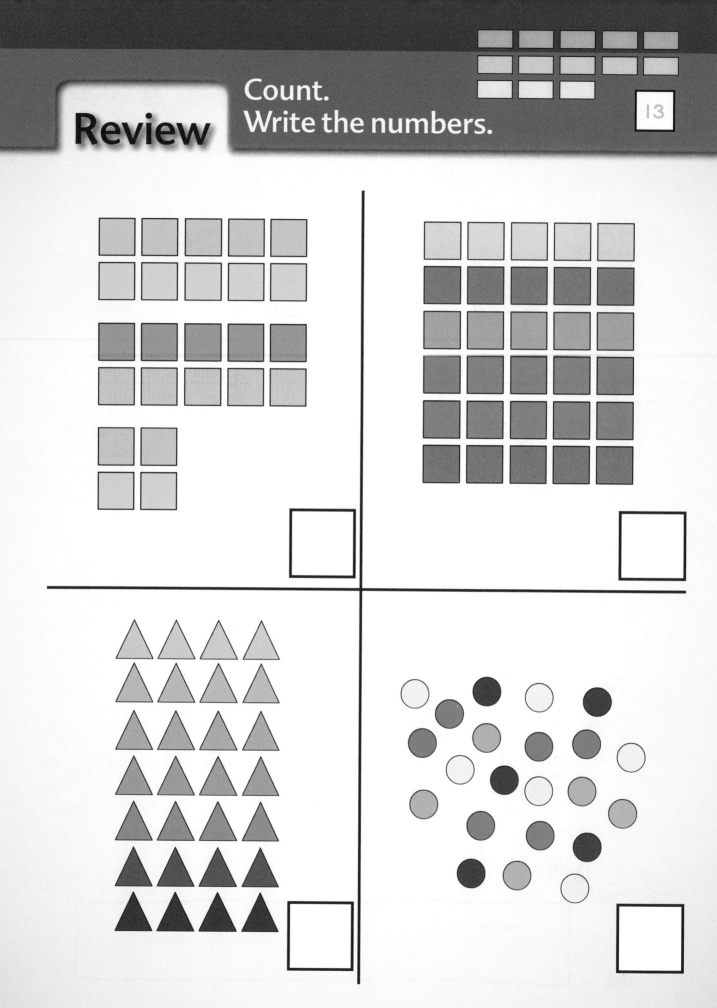

Fill in the missing numbers.

1	2	3	4	5	6		8	9	10
11	12	13	14		16	17	18	19	20
21	22		24	25			28	29	

Write the number that comes before and after the number in the squares.

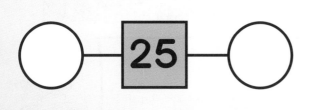

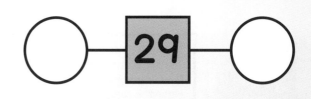

18.1 Look and talk.

Introduction:
Teach the students the action song *If You're Happy and You Know It.*
Development:
Have the students do these actions as they sing the song: 'drink your milk', 'brush your teeth' and 'go to sleep', e.g. "If you're happy and you know it, drink your milk...." Repeat this for 'do wake up', 'brush your teeth', 'eat breakfast' and 'go to school'. Tell the students to look at this page. Use the words '**first**', '**second**', '**third**' and '**fourth**' to describe what the girl and the boy are doing.

Put in order.
Write the numbers.

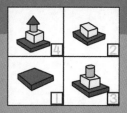

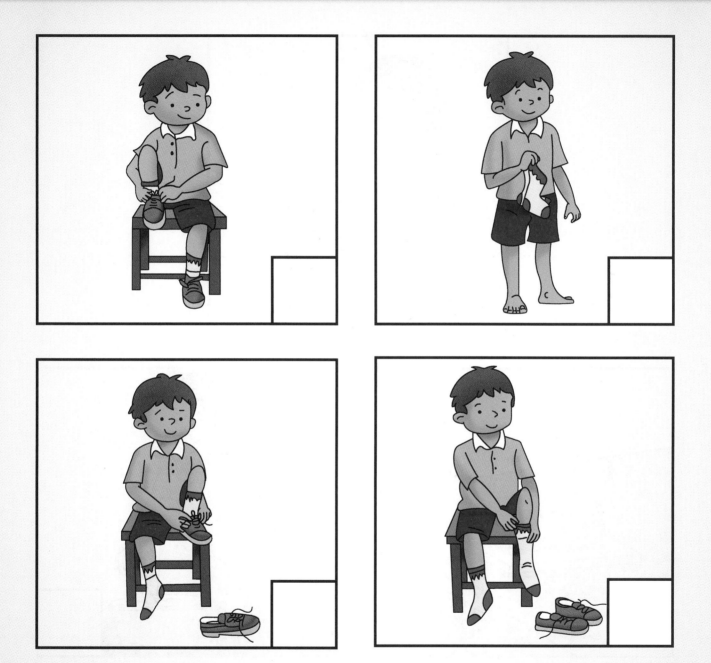

Development:
Have the students take off their shoes and socks. Then ask them to put on their socks and shoes again. Show the numbers 1 to 4 as you use the words 'first', 'second', 'third' and 'fourth' to describe the sequence of events. Have the students look at this page and put the events in the correct order.

Put in order.
Write the numbers.

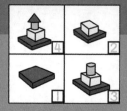

Consolidation:
Have the students look at this page and talk about what the pictures show. Use the words 'first', 'second' and 'third' and show the numbers 1 to 3 at the same time. Have them put the events in the correct order.

Activity I, pages 78-79

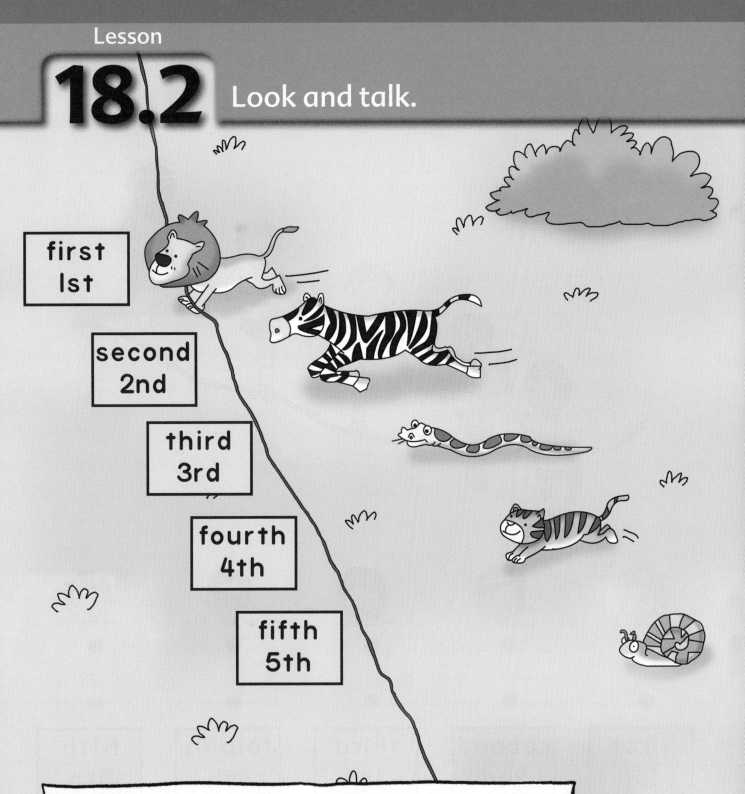

first
1st

second
2nd

third
3rd

fourth
4th

fifth
5th

Introduction:
Have the students name the animals on this page. Ask them to describe the way these animals move and to act out the movements, e.g. walk, run, gallop, crawl, swim, and hop.

Development:
Organize a race among five students. Tell the students to use the words '**first**', '**second**', '**third**', '**fourth**' and '**fifth**' to describe the order in which the students finish. Show the numbers 1 to 5 each time. Repeat this with other students. Have the students look at this page. Encourage them to predict the order in which the animals will finish the race. Accept all reasonable responses. Write the words 'first' to 'fifth' as well as the notations **1st**, **2nd**, **3rd**, **4th** and **5th** on the board. Point to the word or notation each time the word is used.

Match.

first **1st**	**second** **2nd**	**third** **3rd**	**fourth** **4th**	**fifth** **5th**

Development:
Have the students look at this page and predict the order in which the five boys will finish the race. Accept all reasonable responses. Use the words 'first' to 'fifth' to describe the order. Point to the word or notation each time. Tell the students to match each boy's face with the position he is likely to finish in.

Do these pictures show day or night? Match.

Introduction:
Have the students sing a song related to a particular time of the day, e.g. *Are You Sleeping Brother John*?

Development:
Have the students work in groups. Give them the picture cards of several events. Introduce the words '**morning**', '**afternoon**' and '**evening**'. Tell the students to sort the cards into three groups: things we do in the morning, afternoon or evening. Have different students describe what they do in the morning, afternoon or evening.

What do you do at these times?
Draw.

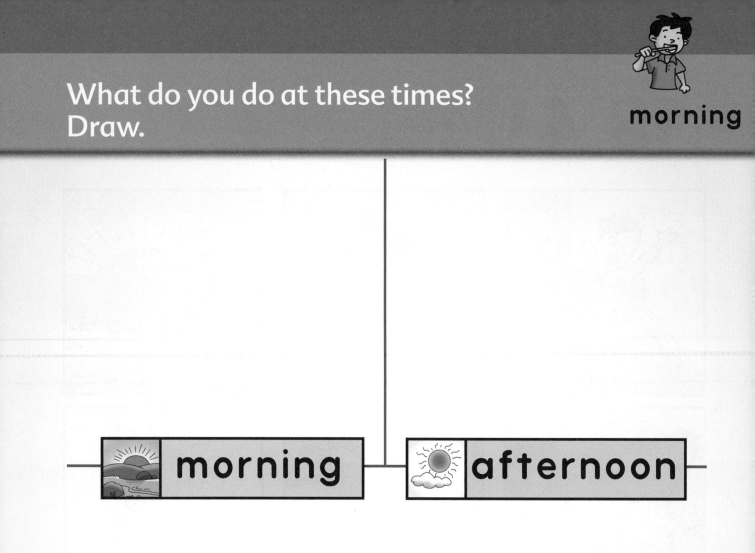

morning | afternoon

evening

Development:
Say the words 'morning', 'afternoon' and 'evening' and tell the students to point to each word on this page. Tell them to describe what they do by drawing. Have them tell each other what they do in the morning, afternoon or evening.

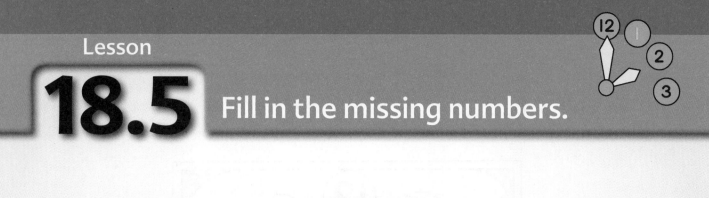

Introduction:
Have the students recite rhymes such as *One, Two, Buckle My Shoe* to review the order of numbers.
Development:
Prepare a few sets of the numeral cards 1 to 12. Give each student a numeral card. At the blow of a whistle, ask them to arrange themselves in order in a circle. Repeat this a few times. Give each student a different numeral card each time. Next, have the students work in groups. Give each group a stack of numeral cards. Tell the groups to arrange the numeral cards in order in a circle. Have the students look at this page. Tell them to fill in the missing numbers. Then, have them to read the numbers on the **clock** face.

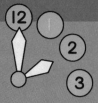

Fill in the missing numbers.

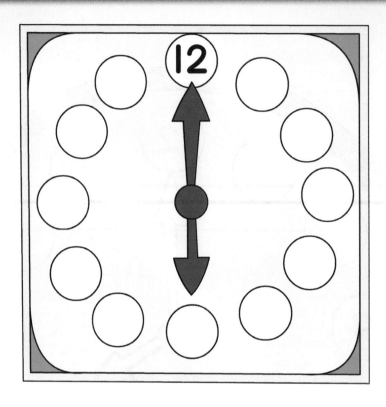

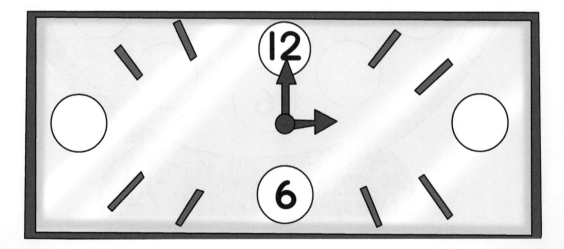

Consolidation:
Have the students complete this page independently. Then, ask them to read the numbers on the clock faces.

Activity 2, pages 80-81

Development:
Use a clock to show 7 **o' clock**. Have the students tell you which is the shorter hand and what number it points to. Then, ask them to tell you which is the longer hand and what number it points to. Tell them that the clock shows 7 o'clock. Repeat with more examples. Next, have the students work in pairs. Tell the students to look at this page. Have each student tell his or her partner what time each clock shows. Ensure that students take turns to do so. Encourage them to talk about what they usually do at that time. Show the students some examples on a digital clock.

Tell the time.

o' clock

o' clock

o' clock

o' clock

o' clock

o' clock

o' clock

o' clock

Consolidation:
Guide the students tell the time on each clock. Then, tell them to write the answers on this page.

Activity 3, page 82

yesterday

today

tomorrow

Development:
Have the students talk about the things they did **yesterday** and what they will be doing **today** and **tomorrow**. Point to the words on this page as you use 'yesterday', 'today' and 'tomorrow'. Have the students look at this page. Tell them to imagine that it is Christmas Eve today. Have them tell you what the people in the picture did yesterday (They went shopping for presents.) and what day it will be tomorrow (Christmas Day). Encourage them to talk about what people do on these days.

Draw 3 things you did yesterday.

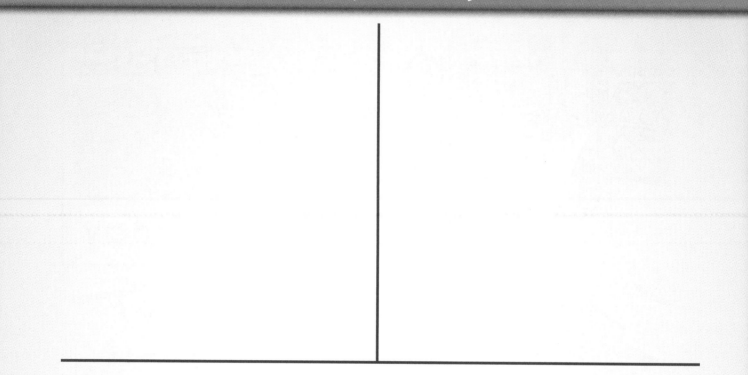

Development:
Tell the students to draw what they did yesterday. Have them work in pairs and tell each other what they have drawn. Conduct a sharing session. Ask, "What did you do yesterday? What did you do today? What will you be doing today/tomorrow?"

Lesson

18.8

What did Nina and her family do? Look and talk.

Monday

Tuesday

Wednesday

Thursday

Friday

Saturday

Sunday

Development:
A few days before this lesson, ask the class, "What day is it today?" Have the students say, e.g. "It is Monday today." Do this on a daily basis. On the day of this lesson, tell the students to look at this page. Say, "Monday" and have the students repeat after you. Tell them to look at the word. Encourage them to use the word as they talk about the activity shown for Monday. Repeat this for the other days.

When did Nina do these?
Match to show the correct day.

• ———— • Saturday

• • **Monday**

• **Tuesday**

• **Wednesday**

• • **Thursday**

• **Friday**

• **Saturday**

• • **Sunday**

Development:
Give each student a card showing a different **day** of the week. Tell the students to group themselves according to the days of the week. Have the students look at page 127. Have each group talk about the event shown for that day. Then, have the students complete this page independently.

What day is it?
Match.

today

tomorrow

yesterday

- • Monday

- • Tuesday

- • Wednesday

- • Thursday

- • Friday

- • Saturday

- • Sunday

Development:
Write a day of the week on the board. Guide the students to name the days that come after. Repeat this a few times with different days. Have the students look at this page. Read the words for them. Encourage them to repeat after you. Then, have the students complete this page independently.

January

February

December

November

October

September

Introduction:
Have the students talk about their favorite summer activities.
Development:
Have the students talk about the activities they do in the different **seasons**. Ask them to look at both pages and to describe the activities shown for each **month**.

Look and talk.

March

April

May

June

August

July

Development:
Have the students work in groups to sort the activities according to seasons. Give the students cards with the names of the months. Have them work in groups to match each picture on this page with a month. Finally, show the class a card, e.g. 'July'. Then, ask them to name the months that come **after**. Repeat this a few times with different months.

Activity 4, page 83

September

December

June

March

Development:
Put up cards with the names of the months. Tell each student to collect a card that shows his or her birthday month. Guide the students to group themselves according to birthday months. Draw a graph on the board showing how many students share the same birthday month. Have the students look at this page. Read the names of the months. Encourage the students to read aloud with you. Have them describe what they see in each picture.

Match each child to his or her birthday month.

- January
- February
- March
- April
- May
- June
- July
- August
- September
- October
- November
- December

Me!

Development:
Ask each student to tell you the month of a classmate's birthday. Have the students say, "Kelly's birthday is in ..." Next, read the words on this page. Encourage the students to repeat after you. Tell the students to attach a photograph of themselves or draw their face in the box provided. Then, have them complete this page in pairs.

May

Sunday	Monday	Tuesday	Wednesday	Thursday	Friday	Saturday
		1	2	3	4	5
6	7	8	9	10	11	12
13	14	15	16	17	18	19
20	21	22	23	24	25	26
27	28	29	30	31		

Introduction:
Ask the students to bring a **calendar** to class. Allow them to talk about the scenes or pictures on their calendars.
Development:
Ask the students to tell you what they see on their calendars. Lead them to notice how the numbers on a calendar are in order. Have the students work in groups. Give them a stack of numeral cards for 1 to 31. Tell them to arrange these cards in order on a five-by-seven grid. Tell them that they have made a calendar. Show a similar arrangement on the board. Omit a few numbers. Have the students say what these numbers are.

Complete the calendar.
Write the numbers in the boxes.

June

Sunday	Monday	Tuesday	Wednesday	Thursday	Friday	Saturday
					1	2
☐	4	☐	6	7	☐	☐
☐	☐	12	13	☐	15	16
☐	18	19	20	21	☐	23
☐	☐	☐	27	28	☐	30

Consolidation:
Have the students look at this page. Guide the students to say what the missing numbers are. Then, tell them to write the numbers in the boxes. Point to a row on the calendar and ask, "This is a row of numbers. How many numbers are there in a row?" Lead them to see that there are seven numbers in each row.

18.12 Look and talk.

July

Sunday	Monday	Tuesday	Wednesday	Thursday	Friday	Saturday
1	2	3	4	5	6	7
8	9	10	11	12	13	14
15	16	17	18	19	20	21
22	23	24	25	26	27	28
29	30	31				

Introduction:
Ask the students what they have been doing the last week.
Development:
Give each student a monthly planner for this month. Show the students what day it is today. Remind the students of two recent events that they participated in. Guide them to look for the dates of these events. Name two upcoming events. Point to the monthly planner as you show them the dates.
Have the students look at this page. Read the days of the week. Encourage them to repeat after you. Show them how to tell the day for each event by moving down the rows. Encourage them to tell you the day for the events recorded on the monthly planner.

What day is it?
Check (✔) the correct box.

	Monday			Thursday			Tuesday
	Wednesday			Saturday			Monday

Development:
Guide the students to read the days of the week on this page. Help them to find the day of the week for each event. Then, ask them to choose the correct day for each event.

18.13 Look and talk.

Introduction:
Create a giant calendar of the current month on the board. Guide the students to fill in the dates and days.

Development:
Point to the calendar as you ask, "What comes after this date?" Repeat with a few more dates. Later, ask, "What day is the 3rd? What day is the 4th?" Finally, talk about the day after the last day of the month. Lead the students to understand that the dates continue on the next page of the calendar. Have the students look at this page. Lead them to see that the 3rd is followed by the 4th and the 31st (or 30th) is followed by the 1st of the next month.

What day comes next?
Say.

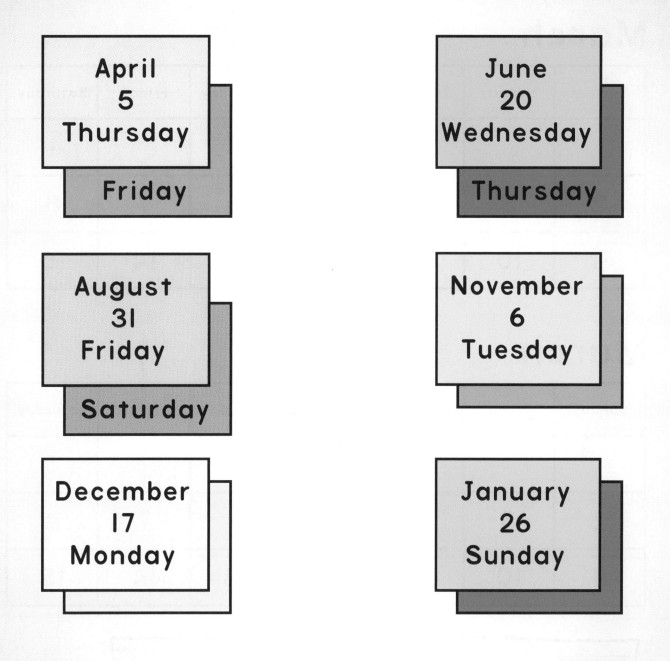

April
5
Thursday

Friday

June
20
Wednesday

Thursday

August
31
Friday

Saturday

November
6
Tuesday

December
17
Monday

January
26
Sunday

Development:
Give the students a few blank cards. Show them a date. Tell them to write the numbers
to show the date of the next day. Have the students look at this page. Guide them
to say the date of the next day. Finally, guide them to tell you the day of the week
following the ones shown.

March

Sunday	Monday	Tuesday	Wednesday	Thursday	Friday	Saturday
						1
2	3	4	5	6	7	8
9	10		12	13	14	15

March

Sunday	Monday	Tuesday	Wednesday	Thursday	Friday	Saturday
						1
2	3	4	5	6	7	8
9	10	11	12	13	14	15

Introduction:
Tell the students to look at the giant calendar they have previously created. Point to the date for today and yesterday. Have the students talk about any interesting events on these days.

Development:
Tell the students to look at the 18th. Get them to tell you the date of the next day. Say, "The day after the 18th is the 19th." Ask, "What is the day **before** the 19th?" Then, tell them to look at the 17th and say, "17th, 18th and 19th." Repeat this with another date. Have the students look at this page. Ask, "What is the date after the 10th?" and "What is the date before the 12th? Get them to check. Then, ask them to say, "10th, 11th, 12th."

What day comes next? Say.

November

Sunday	Monday	Tuesday	Wednesday	Thursday	Friday	Saturday
						1
2	3	4	5	6	7	8
9	10	11	12	13	14	15
16	17	18		20	21	22
	24	25	26	27	28	29
30						

Consolidation:
Have the students tell you the numbers hidden by the snail and the bug. Then, guide them to say the dates of three days in a row, e.g. 18th, 19th and 20th; 23rd, 24th and 25th.

What day comes before?
Say.

January

Sunday	Monday	Tuesday	Wednesday	Thursday	Friday	Saturday
		1	2	3		5
6	7	8	9	10	11	12
13	14	15	16	17	18	19
20	21	22	23	24	25	26
27	28	28	30	31		

September

Sunday	Monday	Tuesday	Wednesday	Thursday	Friday	Saturday
	1	2	3	4	5	
7	8	9	10	11	12	13
14	15	16	17	18	19	20
21	22	23	24	25	26	27
28	29	30				

Consolidation:
Have the students look at this page. Ask them, "What day comes before the 5th?
What is the date? What day is it?" Reinforce and say, "The 4th comes before the 5th.
The 5th comes after the 4th." Repeat this for other examples.

Put in order.
Write the numbers.

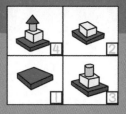

Do and find the answers.

1. **What time of the day is it? Circle the word.**

morning

afternoon

evening

night

2. **Look at a clock. What time is it now?**

It is ☐ o' clock.

3. **Use a calendar. What day is it today?**

4. **Use a calendar. What day is Halloween?**

Instructions:
Tasks 2, 3 and 4 are practical tasks. For task 2, show the students a clock. Have them tell the time by the hour. Tell them to write the number in the box on this page. For task 3, show the students a calendar. Point to the date for today. Have them say what day it is. For task 3, show the students a calendar with the date for Halloween circled. Then, have students say what day it is.

Look and talk.

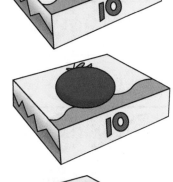

Development:
Put ten pebbles in a transparent container. Have the students count to confirm the number of pebbles. Then, show them containers each with about 50, 70 and 100 pebbles. Ask them to guess the number of pebbles in each container. Encourage the students to share the reasoning for their guesses. Next, prepare a few boxes of pebbles. Put ten pebbles in a closed box. Have the students work in groups. Give each group one box of pebbles. Let them shake the box. Ask the students to guess how many pebbles there are in the box. Tell the students to open the box and find out for themselves. Have some groups bring their boxes to the front. Ask the students, "How many pebbles are there in one box? How many boxes are there? How many pebbles are there altogether?" Guide the students to **count by tens**. Tell them to look at this page and count by tens as they point at the boxes.

Count by 10's.
Fill in the missing numbers.

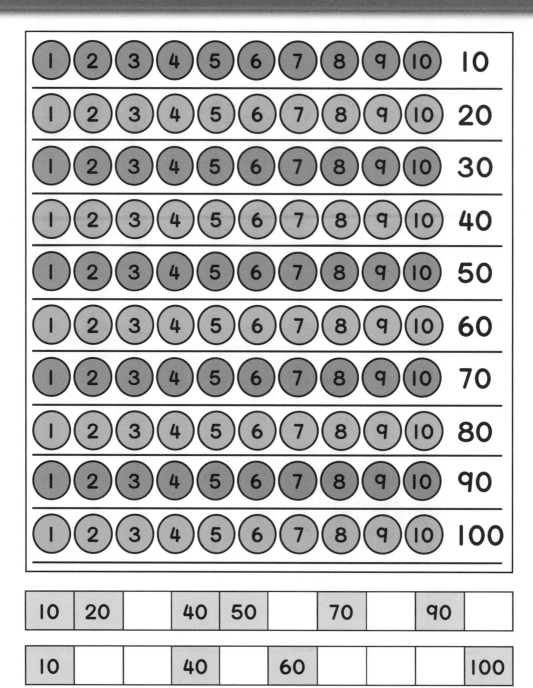

10	20		40	50		70		90	

10			40		60				100

Development:
Show the students numeral cards showing 10, 20, 30, ... 100 as they count by tens. Tell them to look at this page. Ask them to count by tens as they point at each row. Get them to look at the numbers written at the end of each row. Next, place numeral cards showing multiples of ten around the room. Ask the students to look at the first row at the bottom of this page. Tell them to look for the missing numbers by pointing to the cards in the room. Ask them to read the numbers in order. Repeat this for the second row.

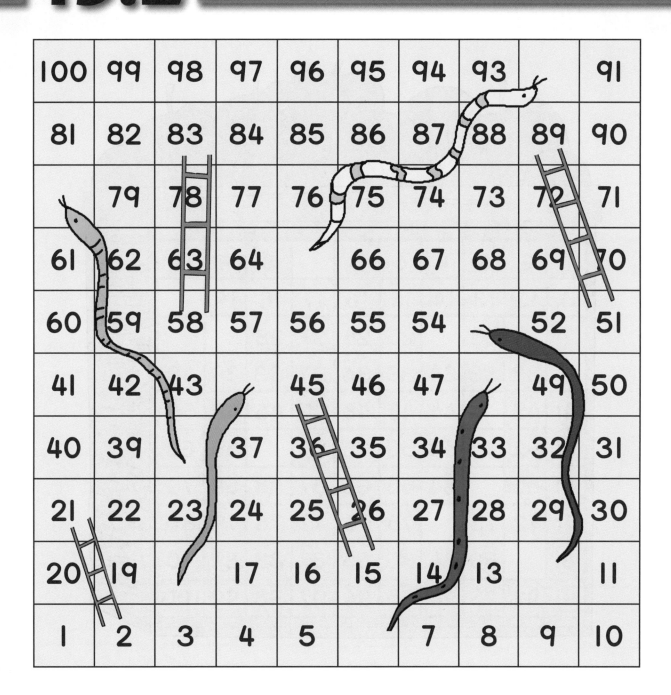

100	99	98	97	96	95	94	93		91
81	82	83	84	85	86	87	88	89	90
	79	78	77	76	75	74	73	72	71
61	62	63	64		66	67	68	69	70
60	59	58	57	56	55	54		52	51
41	42	43		45	46	47		49	50
40	39		37	36	35	34	33	32	31
21	22	23	24	25	26	27	28	29	30
20	19		17	16	15	14	13		11
1	2	3	4	5		7	8	9	10

Introduction:
Let the students play a game of Snakes and Ladders.
Development:
Ask the students to tell you what the missing numbers on this page are.

Fill in the missing numbers.
Then read the numbers.

1	2	3	4	5	6		8	9	10
11	12	13	14	15	16	17	18	19	
21		23		25	26	27	28		
	32	33	34	35	36	37	38	39	40
41	42		44	45	46	47	48	49	50
51	52		54	55	56	57		59	60
61	62		64	65	66	67	68	69	70
71	72	73		75	76	77	78	79	80
81		83	84	85	86	87	88	89	90
91	92	93	94	95	96	97	98	99	100

Introduction:
Tell the students to look at this page. Ask them to look at the incomplete chart and talk about the numbers and any patterns they notice.
Development:
Have the students tell you what the missing numbers are. Tell them to fill in the missing numbers. Then, ask them to say the numbers as a class.

Activities 1 and 2, pages 86-89

Lesson
19.3
How many fingers are there? Count and write the numbers.

5

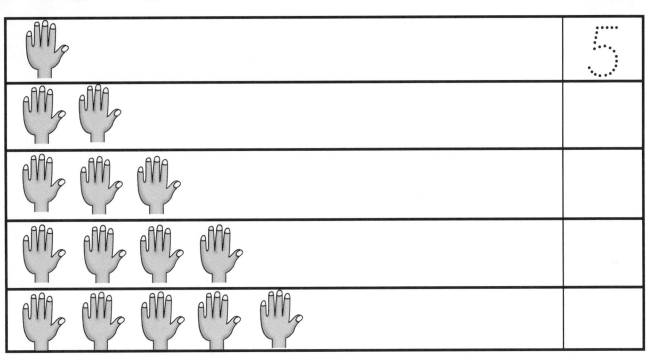

	5

Count by 5's. Circle the correct numbers. Then read them.

1	2	3	4	5	6	7	8	9	10
11	12	13	14	15	16	17	18	19	20
21	22	23	24	25	26	27	28	29	30
31	32	33	34	35	36	37	38	39	40
41	42	43	44	45	46	47	48	49	50

Development:
Get five students to stand in a row. Ask them to raise their right hand one at a time. Tell the class to count the number of fingers by counting on. Emphasize the multiples of five. Guide the students to **count by fives** up to 25. Get them to complete the table on this page. Then, tell the students to sit in a circle. Ask them to clap their hands. Tell them to count silently but to say the multiples of five aloud. Get one student to start by saying "Five" and the next to continue. Encourage them to count to 100. Tell them to look at this page. Tell them to count silently as they point at the numbers but to say the multiples of five aloud. Ask them to circle these numbers. Get the class to count by fives up to 100 as they look at the numbers they have circled.

Count by 5's.
Write the numbers.

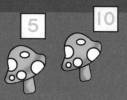

Introduction:
Ask the students to count the number of spots on each mushroom. Have them say what they notice.
Development:
Tell the students to count by fives as they write the numbers on this page. Students who need to use the spots to help them count may do so. Finally, ask the students, e.g. "What number does the tortoise have?" Call for volunteers to answer these questions.

1	2	3	4	5	6	7	8	9	10
11	12	13	14	15	16	17	18	19	20
21	22	23	24	25	26	27	28	29	30
31	32	33	34	35	36	37	38	39	40
41	42	43	44	45	46	47	48	49	50
51	52	53	54	55	56	57	58	59	60
61	62	63	64	65	66	67	68	69	70
71	72	73	74	75	76	77	78	79	80
81	82	83	84	85	86	87	88	89	90
91	92	93	94	95	96	97	98	99	100

Development:
Tell the students to sit in a circle. Ask them to clap their hands. Tell them to count silently but to say the multiples of two aloud. Get one student to start by saying, "Two" and the next student to continue. Ask them to look at this page. Tell the students to point at the numbers as they **count by twos** up to 100.

How many shoes are there in each row? Count by 2's. Then write the numbers.

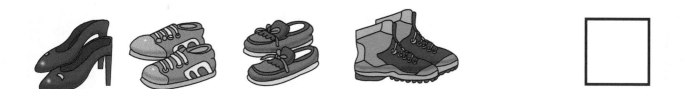

45

58

60

72

Development:
Prepare cards that each show one to ten dots. Give each student a card. Play a game.
Students have to form a group to show the correct number. Demonstrate this. Say a number
between ten and 100. Select students to form a group. If you say 28, then two students each
holding a card with ten dots and one student holding a card with eight dots form a group
and sit down. Play this game a few times. Ensure that every student has a chance to form
a group. Then, tell the students to look at this page. Ask them to count by tens whenever
possible to tell you the numbers shown.

How many  are there?
Count and write the numbers.

5

Development:
Guide the students to complete this page. Say, e.g. "Look at the mushrooms the frog has. How many spots are there?" Then ask, "How many groups of ten spots are there?"
For numbers 29, 31, 57 and 63, emphasize the relationship between the **tens and ones**. Say, e.g. "This number starts with 2." when the students say, "There are two groups of ten spots." Get the class to say, "29 is 2 tens and 9 ones".

Review   Fill in the missing numbers.

1	2	3	4	5	6	7	8	9	10
11	12	13	14	15	16		18	19	20
21	22	23	24	25	26	27	28	29	
31	32	33	34	35	36	37	38	39	40
41	42	43	44	45	46	47	48	49	50
	52	53	54	55	56	57		59	60
61	62	63	64	65	66	67	68	69	70
71	72	73	74	75	76	77			80
81	82	83	84	85	86	87	88	89	90
91	92	93	94	95	96	97	98	99	100

Count by 5's. Write the numbers.
Then count by 2's and write the numbers.

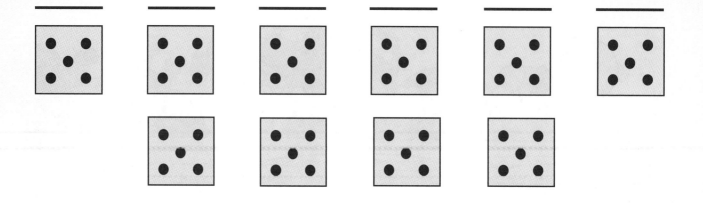

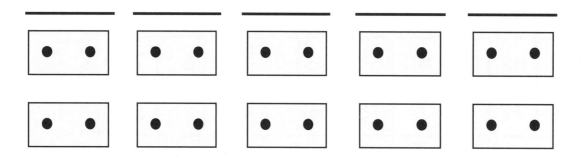

Count.
Write the numbers.

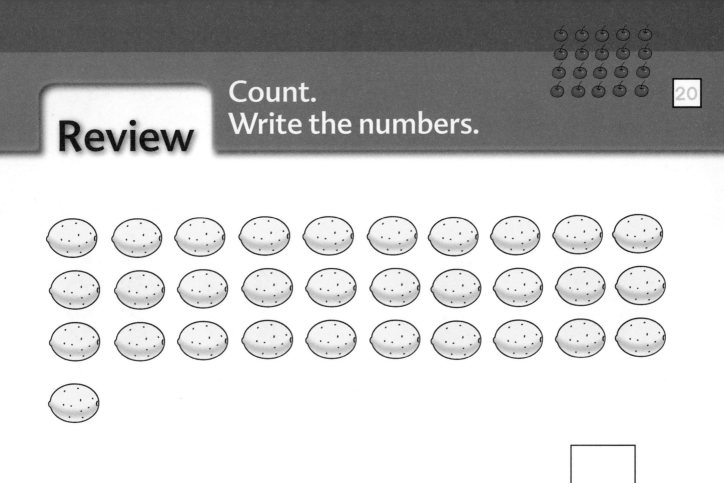

20.1   Look and talk.

penny
1 cent

nickel
5 cents

dime
10 cents

quarter
25 cents

Introduction:
Tell the students that they will be going to a nearby shop to buy things in a week or so.
Get them to think about where they should go, how to get there and so on.
Development:
Give each student one **coin** of each type. Ask the students if they know what they are.
Tell them the names of these coins: **penny (1 cent)**, **nickel (5 cents)**, **dime (10 cents)** and
quarter (25 cents). Have the students work in groups. Tell them to pool their coins and
sort them according to whether they are pennies, nickels, dimes or quarters.

Match.

 •   • 1 cent

(penny) •   • 5 cents

 •   • 10 cents

(quarter) •   • 25 cents

Introduction:
Check that the students are able to read the numerals 1, 5, 10 and 25.
Development:
Divide the students into two groups. Give each student in one group a coin and each student in the other a card with the **value** of a coin (either 1 cent, 5 cents, 10 cents or 25 cents) printed on it. Ensure that there is a match for every card. Tell the students to find a partner so that the coin matches the value shown on the card. Guide the students to work on this page.

20.2 Look and talk.

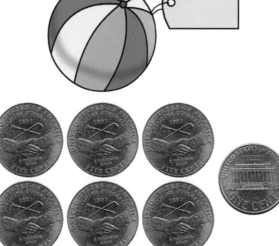

Development:
Show the students a few pennies and ask them to guess if the amount is more or less than 10 cents. Show them a few nickels and ask them, "Do you think this is more or less than 50 cents?" Repeat this using dimes and quarters. Guide the students to count the exact amount by **counting by ones** (for the pennies), **by tens** (for the dimes) and **by fives** (for the nickels). Next, show a few coins of two different denominations and ask them to guess the amount. Guide the students to count the exact amount by counting by tens and ones (for dimes and pennies) or by fives and ones (for nickels and pennies). Tell the students to look at this page. Have them count the coins to tell the price of each item. Write the numerals on the board to emphasize the value of the coins.

5¢ 10¢

How much money is there?
Write the amount.

15 cents

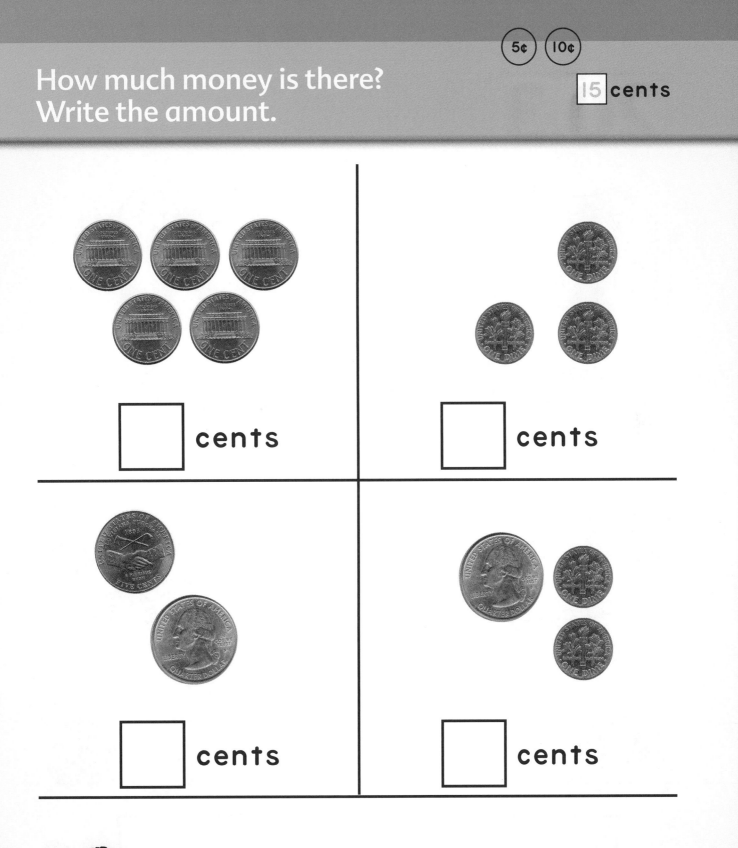

[ ] cents

[ ] cents

[ ] cents

[ ] cents

Development:
Guide the students to count the coins on this page. Emphasize counting all by ones
(for 5 cents), counting all by tens (for 30 cents), counting on by fives (for 30 cents) and
counting on by tens (for 45 cents). Each time, tell the students to write the value and
read the amount, e.g. "45 cents."

20.3 How much does it cost? Match.

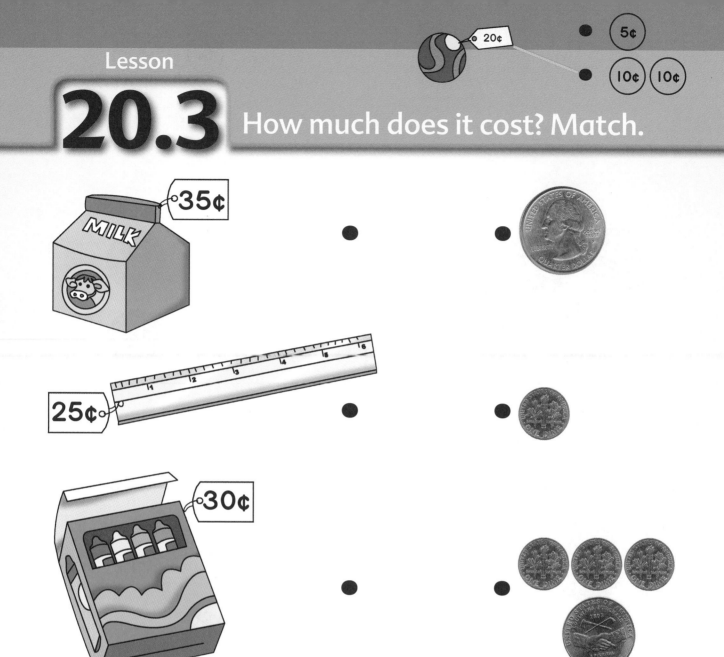

Introduction:
Tell the students a story about a boy who goes on an adventure. Along the way he encounters unfamiliar situations that the students can help with.

Development:
Tell the students that the boy wanders into a shop and sees what the students see on this page. The boy finds the symbol ¢ unfamiliar. Ask the students to help. Tell the students to read the prices on the price tags. Then lead them to match each tag with the correct set of coins. Emphasize counting all by tens and counting on by fives for two of the situations. Use real coins to help students as they count.

Write the price.

163
one hundred sixty-three

Activity 2, page 95

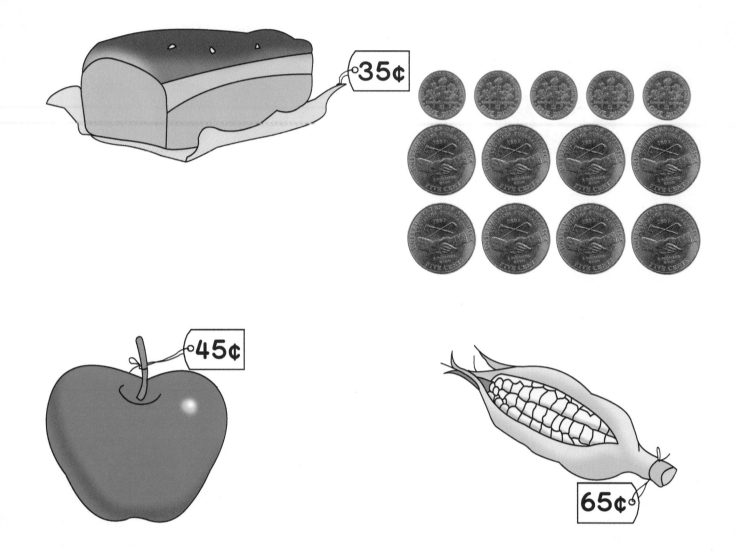

35¢

45¢

65¢

Introduction:
Tell the students how they can ask for the price of something politely.
Development:
Have the students tell the prices of items on this page. Give them five dimes and eight nickels to pay for each of the three items. Emphasize counting all and counting on by fives and tens.

Pay for the things.
Circle the coins you need.

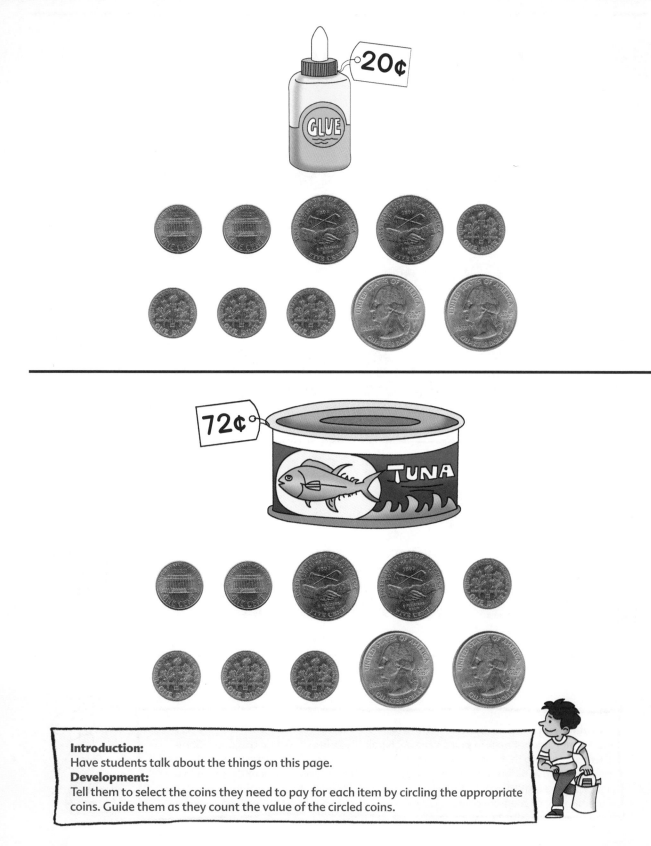

Introduction:
Have students talk about the things on this page.

Development:
Tell them to select the coins they need to pay for each item by circling the appropriate coins. Guide them as they count the value of the circled coins.

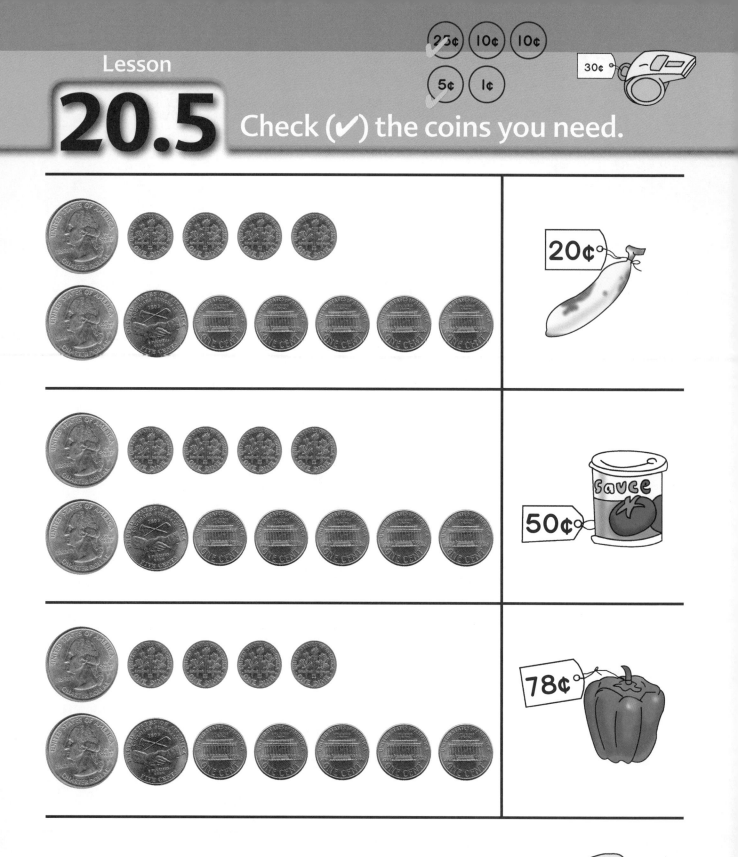

20¢

50¢

78¢

Development:
Have the students work in pairs. Give each pair the coins shown on this page. Show them something that costs 20¢. Tell the students to show their partners how they can pay for it. Have different pairs of students show the different ways to do so. Lead the students see that there are different ways to pay for each item. Get them to practice counting on, or counting all by ones, fives and tens using their classmates' responses.

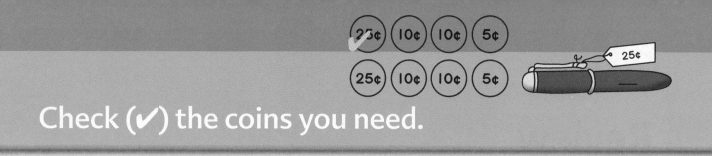

Check (✔) the coins you need.

Consolidation:
Ask the students to work on this page independently. Encourage them to see that there are different ways to pay for each thing.

How much does it cost? Match.

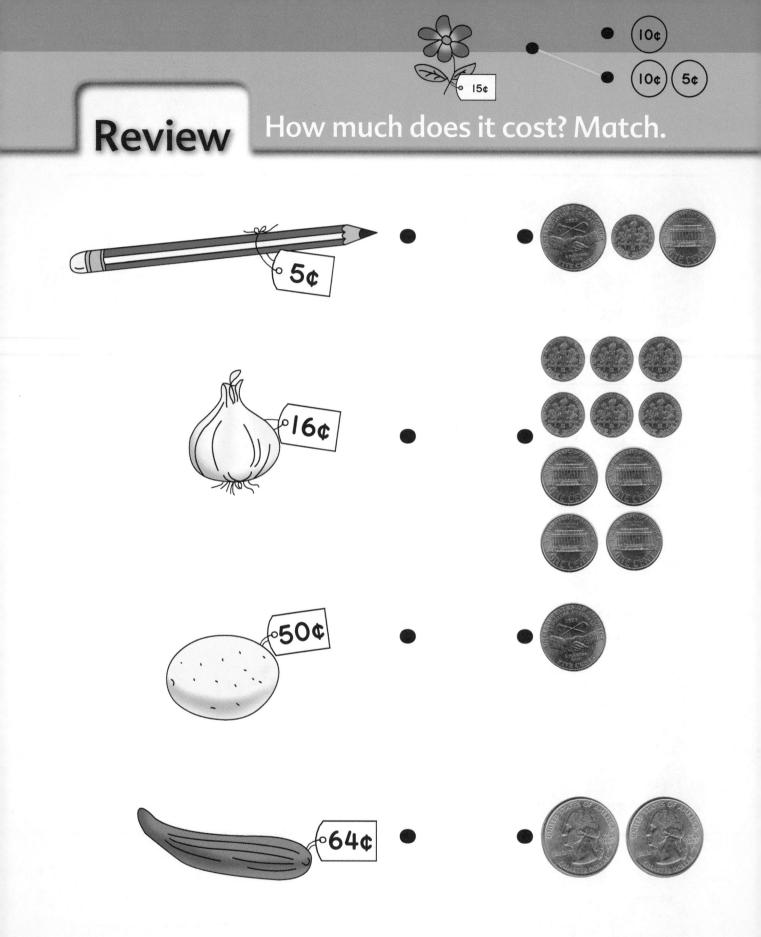

Check (✔) the coins you need.

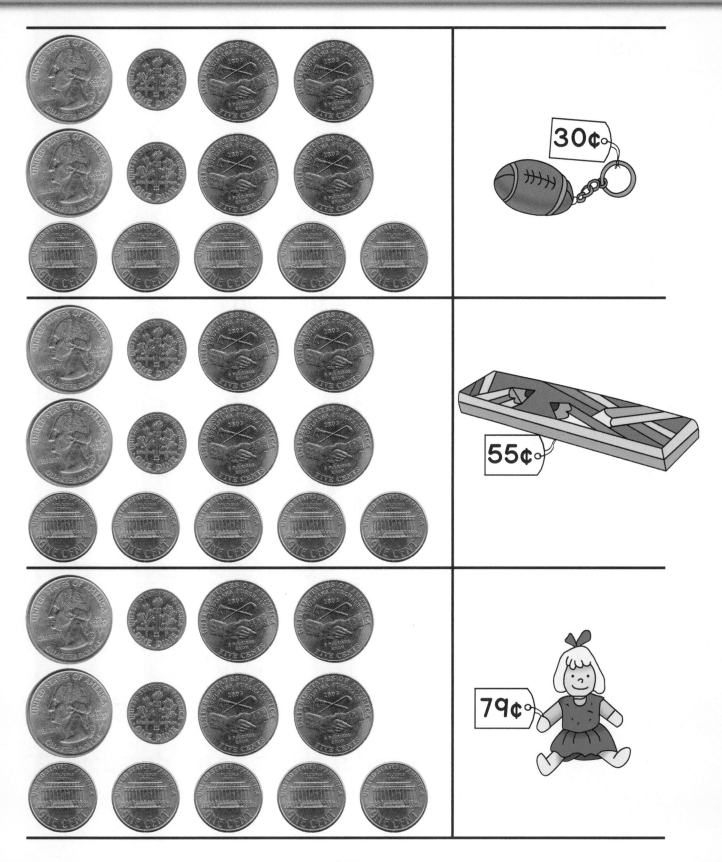

Glossary

Word	Meaning
add	To put together. Example: $3 \quad + \quad 2 \quad = \quad 5$ We write '+' to mean add. There are **5** apples **altogether**.
addition sentence	$1 + 2 = 3 \qquad 3 + 1 = 4$ These are examples of **addition sentences**.
calendar	MONDAY **6** JANUARY TUESDAY **12** FEBRUARY WEDNESDAY **18** MARCH A **calendar** shows us the day, date and month.

Word	Meaning
day	There are **7 days** in a week.

Monday
Tuesday
Wednesday
Thursday
Friday
Saturday
Sunday

count by

We can count things by **10**'s, **5**'s or **2**'s.
For example:
Tens:

10   20   30

Fives:

5   10   15

Twos:

2   4   6

Word	Meaning
count on	We can **count on** to add. Example: 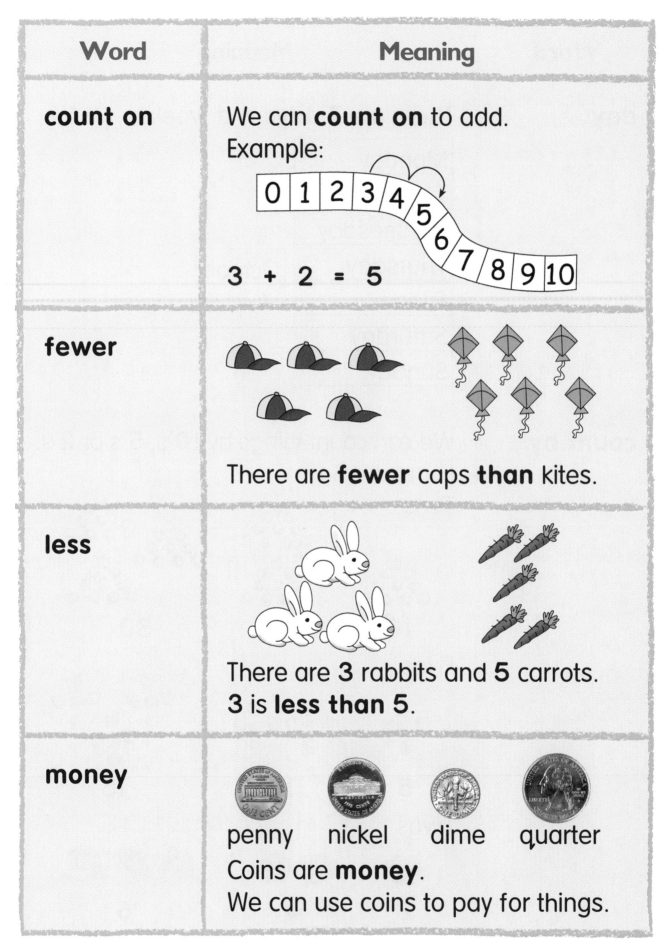 3 + 2 = 5
fewer	There are **fewer** caps **than** kites.
less	There are **3** rabbits and **5** carrots. **3** is **less than 5**.
money	penny nickel dime quarter Coins are **money**. We can use coins to pay for things.

Word	Meaning
month	There are **12** months in a **year**.

January	July
February	August
March	September
April	October
May	November
June	December

more

There are **8** bees and **5** ants.
8 is **more than 5**.

number bonds

Word	Meaning
numbers	These are the numbers **11** to **20**.

11	eleven
12	twelve
13	thirteen
14	fourteen
15	fifteen
16	sixteen
17	seventeen
18	eighteen
19	nineteen
20	twenty

These are the numbers **21** to **30**.

21	twenty-one
22	twenty-two
23	twenty-three
24	twenty-four
25	twenty-five
26	twenty-six
27	twenty-seven
28	twenty-eight
29	twenty-nine
30	thirty

Word	Meaning
place value chart	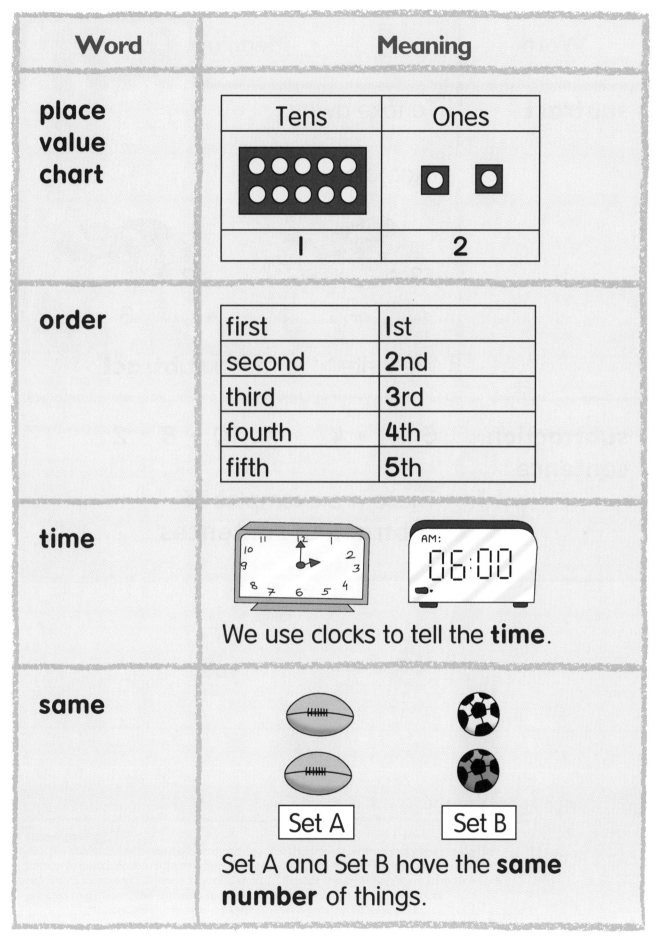
order	first — 1st second — 2nd third — 3rd fourth — 4th fifth — 5th
time	We use clocks to tell the **time**.
same	Set A and Set B have the **same number** of things.

Word	Meaning
subtract	To take away. Example: 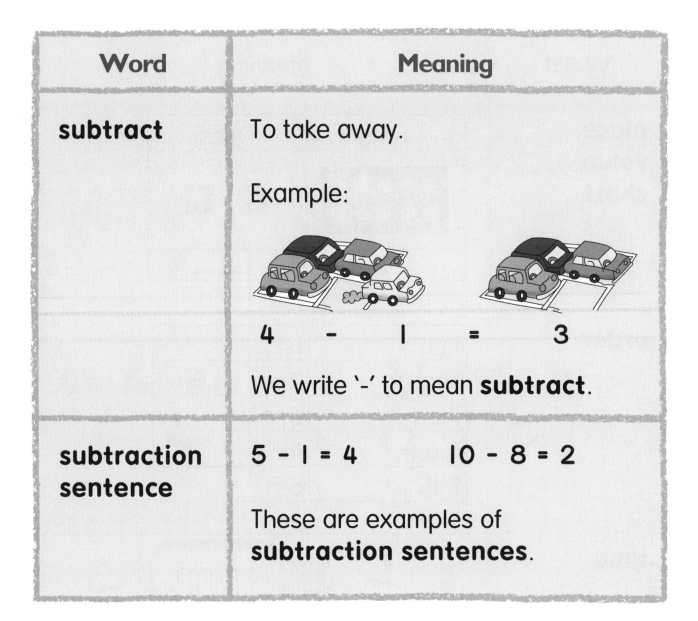 4 - 1 = 3 We write '-' to mean **subtract**.
subtraction sentence	5 - 1 = 4 10 - 8 = 2 These are examples of **subtraction sentences**.

Index

Math at Home

Color the parts with the correct numbers.

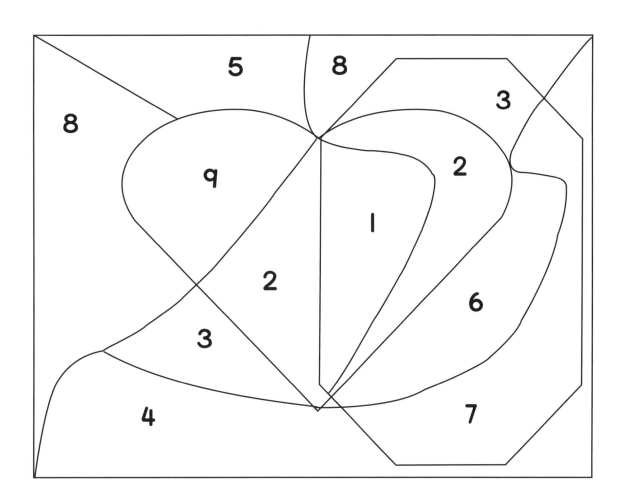

- - - - - - - - - - ✂ -

Development:
Have your child look at the puzzle on this page. Then, ask, "Which number is more than 8?" and "Which numbers are less than 3?" Ask your child to color the parts of the puzzle that contain these numbers. After this activity, create a different puzzle with similar clues for your child to solve. Guide your child to create his or her own puzzles with similar clues.

Blank

Math at Home

Look for the numbers 1 to 20. Make a scrapbook.

Development:
Provide your child with old newspapers, magazines and brochures. Have your child look for the numbers 1 to 20. Help your child to make a scrapbook showing the numbers 1 to 20. For each number, ask your child to draw the correct number of items. For numbers more than 10, tell your child to circle every ten items in the picture.

Blank

Math at Home

Choose a card. Say the correct number to make 10.

Development:
Play a card game with your child. This will help familiarize your child with basic number facts. Remove all picture cards such as Ace, Joker, King, Queen and Jack. Place the stack of cards face down on the table. Have your child choose any card and say the number shown. Then, ask, "What number do you need to make 10?" Repeat this a few times with different numbers. Ensure that the numbers do not add up to more than 10.

Blank

Math at Home

Aim, throw and score!

Development:
Play a ball game with your child. Prepare an empty basket and five balls. Place the basket some distance away. Play 3 rounds. In every round, each player has 5 attempts at throwing the ball. The player scores 1 point when the ball goes into the basket. To keep count, have your child color a ball on page 186 each time a ball goes into the basket. After your child has completed 5 attempts, ask him/her to record your score in the same way as you take your turn to throw. Once you have completed 5 attempts, encourage your child to count the total number of colored balls on page 186. You may wish to make the game more challenging by increasing the distance between the basket and the person who throws the ball.

What is the score?
Color and add.

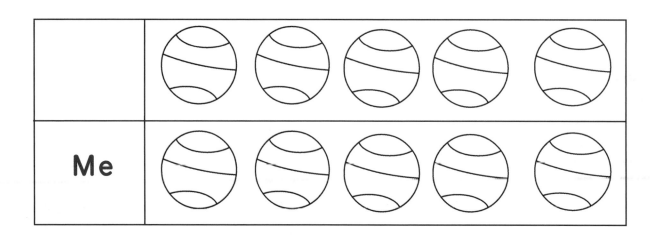

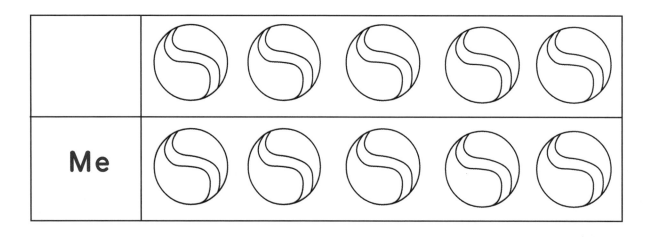

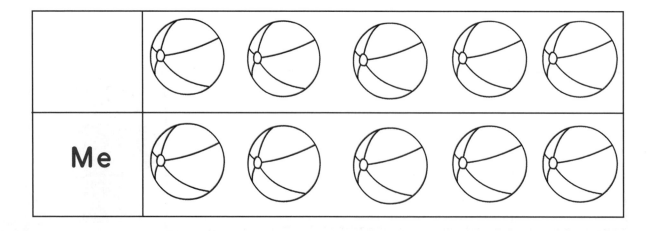

Math at Home

Subtract.
You win if your answer is a number more than the other player's!

Development:
Play a card game with your child. Remove the following cards: Joker, King, Queen and Jack. Keep the Ace cards. Use these to represent the numeral 1. Each player gets 5 cards. Each player selects any 2 cards and subtracts the numbers shown. The aim of the game is to get an answer which you think is a number that is more than the other player's answer. Both players place the cards they have chosen face down on the table. Then, open the cards at the same time. The player with the greater number wins and takes all four cards. Play six rounds. The player with the most cards wins. To make it more challenging, adapt this game for more players.

Blank

Math at Home

Make a clock.

Materials:

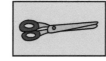

Development:
Help your child to make a paper clock. Prepare the materials: a paper plate, some sheets of colored paper, a pair of scissors, colored pencils and a fastener. Ask, "Where do we write the numbers 12, 3, 6 and 9?" Guide your child to write in the remaining numbers. Guide your child to draw the hour and minute hands on a sheet of paper. Help your child to cut and attach the hands to the clock. Ask your child to show you different times of the day. Ask, "Can you show 10 o'clock? What did you do at 10 o'clock? / What do you want to do at 10 o'clock?" Encourage your child to bring the clock to school.

Math at Home

Whose birthday is it?
Use a calendar to find out.

JUNE
20
FRIDAY

Development:
Help your child to look up a calendar of the current year and find the dates of some family members' or friends' birthdays. Guide your child to identify the day of the week their birthdays fall on. Ask your child to record the information on pages 191 and 192 by pasting photographs or drawing faces in the bigger boxes. Below each box, have your child paste the cutout showing the day each birthday falls on. Cutouts showing the days of the week are provided on page 193.

Attach a photo or draw.
Paste the cutouts to name the days.

Attach a photo or draw.
Paste the cutouts to name the days.

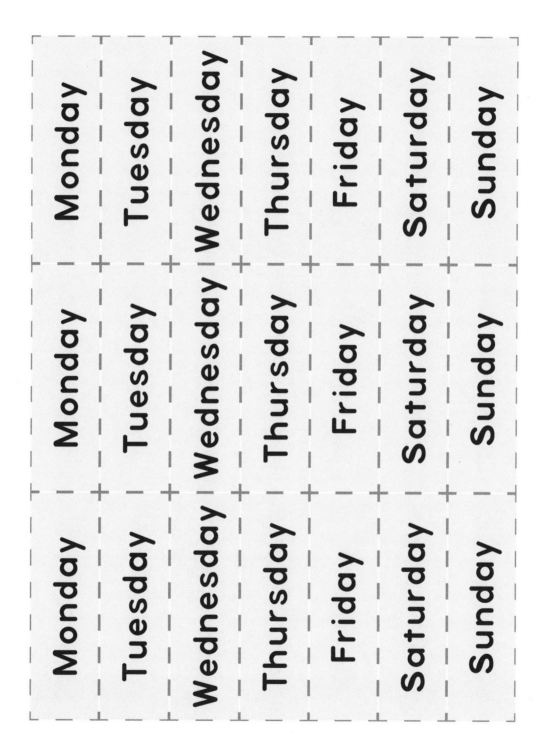

Monday   Monday   Monday

Tuesday   Tuesday   Tuesday

Wednesday   Wednesday   Wednesday

Thursday   Thursday   Thursday

Friday   Friday   Friday

Saturday   Saturday   Saturday

Sunday   Sunday   Sunday

Blank